HEROES OF THE HOLOCAUST

HEROES
OF THE
HOLOCAUST

✳ ✳ ✳ ✳ ✳ ✳ ✳ ✳ ✳ ✳ ✳ ✳ ✳ ✳ ✳

TED GOTTFRIED

Illustrations by Stephen Alcorn

THE HOLOCAUST
Twenty-First Century Books
Brookfield, Connecticut

Chapter opening illustrations and design by Stephen Alcorn © www.alcorngallery.com

Photographs courtesy of © Hulton-Deutsch Collection/Corbis: p. 16; © Chr. Kaiser/Gütersloher Verlagshaus, Gütersloh: p. 27; National Archives/USHMM: pp. 37, 80; Jack Lewis/USHMM: p. 47; Yad Vashem Photo Archives/USHMM: p. 59; Hiroki Sugihara/USHMM: p. 70; Eliyahu Mallenbaum/USHMM: p. 90

Library of Congress Cataloging-in-Publication Data
Gottfried, Ted.
Heroes of the Holocaust / Ted Gottfried.
p. cm. — (The Holocaust)
Includes index.
ISBN 0-7613-1717-1 (lib. bdg.)
1. World War, 1939-1945—Jews—Rescue—Juvenile literature. 2. Righteous Gentiles in the Holocaust—Juvenile literature. 3. World War, 1939-1945—Jewish resistance—Juvenile literature. 4. Holocaust, Jewish (1939-1945)—Juvenile literature. [1. World War, 1939-1945—Jews—Rescue. 2. Righteous Gentiles in the Holocaust. 3. World War, 1939-1945—Jewish resistance. 4. Holocaust, Jewish (1939-1945).] I. Title. II. Holocaust (Brookfield, Conn.)
D804.6.G68   2001   940.53'18—dc21   00-032571

Published by Twenty-First Century Books
A Division of The Millbrook Press, Inc.
2 Old New Milford Road
Brookfield, Connecticut 06804
www.millbrookpress.com

In loving memory
of
Minnie and Sam Groveman
—Peace and Love

ACKNOWLEDGMENTS

I am grateful to personnel of the Judaica Room of the New York Central Research Library, the Mid-Manhattan Library, the Jewish Museum in New York, and the United States Holocaust Memorial Museum in Washington, D. C., as well as those at the central branch of the Queensboro Public Library for their aid in gathering material for this book. Thanks are also due—with much love—to my wife, Harriet Gottfried, who—as always—read and critiqued this book. Her help was invaluable, but any shortcomings in the work are mine alone.

—Ted Gottfried

CONTENTS

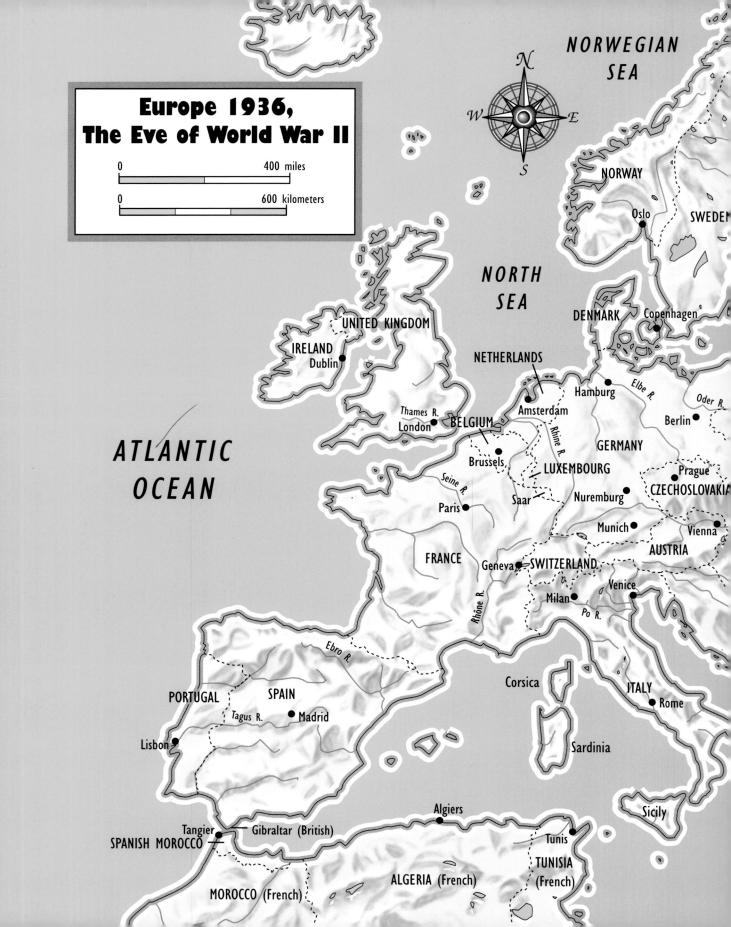

Europe 1936, The Eve of World War II

0   400 miles

0   600 kilometers

NORWEGIAN SEA

N
W · E
S

NORWAY

Oslo

SWEDEN

NORTH SEA

DENMARK

Copenhagen

UNITED KINGDOM

IRELAND
Dublin

NETHERLANDS

Amsterdam

Hamburg

Elbe R.

Oder R.

Berlin

ATLANTIC OCEAN

Thames R.

London

BELGIUM

Brussels

Rhine R.

GERMANY

Prague

CZECHOSLOVAKIA

LUXEMBOURG

Seine R.

Saar

Nuremburg

Paris

Munich

Vienna

FRANCE

Geneva

SWITZERLAND

AUSTRIA

Rhône R.

Venice

Milan

Po R.

Ebro R.

Corsica

ITALY

PORTUGAL

SPAIN

Tagus R.

Madrid

Rome

Lisbon

Sardinia

Algiers

Sicily

Tangier

Gibraltar (British)

Tunis

SPANISH MOROCCO

TUNISIA (French)

ALGERIA (French)

MOROCCO (French)

THE ROAD TO GENOCIDE

1

The mass murder of six million European Jews in World War II is inconceivable to many people today. If evil on such a large scale can take place, what hope is there for goodness and morality? The answer—the hope—may well lie with the heroes of the Holocaust who risked their lives for others because, in the words of one of them, "How else should one react when a human life is endangered?"[1]

The Soil of Genocide

These are the stories of those Holocaust heroes. The circumstances forging their heroism began in November 1918, at the end of World War I. Germany was a defeated nation on the brink of starvation. War had destroyed the country's merchant fleet and transportation system. There was no way to get food to the people. That winter many Germans died of starvation.

Germany's postwar government was in turmoil. There were no jobs. German money had no value. The Treaty of Versailles, signed June 28, 1919, forced Germany to give up one seventh of its territory, including the coal-rich Saar region, other manufacturing areas, and all of its overseas colonies. The resulting unrest and hardship persisted into the 1920s.

The suffering German people blamed the Treaty of Versailles for depriving them of a way to recover their prosperity. Some blamed the government for not relieving their hardship. Some blamed the bankers for devaluing German currency. Some blamed the manufacturers for cutting their workforces. Some blamed the trade unions for not standing up to the factory owners. And some blamed the Jews for all of the above and more.

Like many European countries, Germany had a history of anti-Semitism (hatred of Jews). Now the bitterness of the times provided fertile ground for it. The Nazis would seed that ground, and the world would reap the devastating consequences.

The Origins of Nazism

From the first, the Nazi party was anti-Semitic. It began as the Committee of Independent Workmen opposed to communism and trade unions. In January 1919 the committee merged with the Political Workers Circle. The new group called itself the National Socialist German Workers', or Nazi, party.

In September 1919 a twenty-nine-year-old former German army corporal who was already a committed anti-Semite joined the new Nazi party. His name was Adolf Hitler. The following February the party released a twenty-five-point party program, which Hitler had been instrumental in formulating. Point Four defined German citizenship as follows: "Only those of German blood, whatever their creed, may be members of the nation. Accordingly no Jew may be a member of the nation."[2]

The Nazis were not the only anti-Semites in Germany at that time. Between 1919 and 1923, "a large number of government reports from around Germany" spoke of "a virulent hatred of Jews."[3] Nor were the Jews alone in being targeted by the Nazis. They were only the first of many ethnic groups to be labeled inferior by Hitler.

The Aryans

In *Mein Kampf* (*My Struggle*), Hitler's combination of autobiography and Nazi theory, he called these groups *Untermenschen*—subhumans. They included Slavs

(Poles, Serbs, and Russians among others), southern Europeans, and all non-white races. The German people were members of the Aryan race, and this race was superior to all others, according to Hitler.

He regarded European civilization as having been created by Aryans. In his view, civilization was the result of Aryan invasions in which inferior nations were conquered and their subjects ruled by Aryans. Historically, according to Hitler, Aryans had always been the masters and their inferiors the slaves. Now Germany's salvation demanded that this master-slave relationship be reinstituted.

Aryans, by his definition, must always maintain the purity of their race. In his distorted version of history, Germans had never mixed their blood with the blood of others. Never must they do so in the future. He declared that all other people were mongrels. According to Hitler, the Germans—the Aryans—alone were pure of blood and noble of spirit. Only they deserved to be the masters of humankind.

By the time Hitler came to power in 1933, his views of Aryan superiority were Nazi doctrine and had considerable support among the German people. The first to be targeted as *Untermenschen* were the 500,000 Jews of Germany. The genocide of other European Jews would follow.

European Anti-Semitism

The Jews were a Semitic people who originated in the Middle East. Their mass exodus from that region was provoked by a series of religious wars between the empires of Islam and the Christian crusaders. Between the sixth century A.D. and the sixteenth century, the minority Jewish population was targeted as heathen by all sides. Originally they fled to Spain and Portugal. Then, as they were singled out as nonbelievers by the Spanish Inquisition, the Jews escaped to France, the Netherlands, Belgium, and Italy. When the Inquisition moved on to those countries, the Jews sought sanctuary in the independent states that would one day become Germany, as well as in Austria, Hungary, and nations to the east such as Poland and Russia.

In these countries Jews stood out as strange and different from the local population. They were regarded as intruders. They worshiped differently. They dressed differently, wearing skullcaps and prayer shawls. Their customs were different. Often set apart by laws that restricted their activities and herded them into ghettos, they did not assimilate easily.

When the Jews arrived in most of these countries, the land was already owned. There were more than enough peasants to farm it. Skilled artisans barred Jews from entering their trades. Of necessity, the Jews became merchants and shopkeepers. Through travel and contacts with relatives in other places, they were familiar with the various European currencies. Many of them became money changers, who provided a valued service to those who transported goods for sale from one country to another. This led to some Jews becoming money-lenders, and subsequently bankers.

Because of their involvement with money, Jews became a target for the dis-content of the poor. Bizarre rumors spread that Jews killed Christian children and used their blood in rituals. Other wild stories circulated. Then, in 1897, the Russian secret police forged a document called *The Protocols of the Learned Elders of Zion*. Its purpose was to redirect the wrath of the downtrodden peas-ants from the czarist government to the Jews. The *Protocols* claimed that Jews planned "to disrupt Christian civilization and erect a world state under their joint rule. . . . If subversion failed, all the capitals of Europe were to be sabo-taged."[4]

Sparked by the *Protocols*, waves of pogroms (anti-Jewish massacres) swept Russia, Poland, and other Eastern European countries. Translations of the *Protocols* spread to Central and Western Europe. In Austria, Jews were attacked and savagely beaten. In France, Alfred Dreyfus, a Jewish army officer, was falsely accused of treason amid mounting anti-Semitism. In 1920s Germany a Nazi group murdered prominent Jews, including Walter Rathenau, the foreign

A symbol of Nazi persecution, this wall separates the Jewish ghetto in Warsaw, Poland, from the rest of the city.

minister of the newly formed German Republic. By the time Hitler came to power in the 1930s the *Protocols* had circulated widely, and anti-Semitism was a fact of life in Germany and most other European countries.

The Conquest of Europe

Hitler's long-term goal as Führer (leader) of Germany was to expand the territory of the German nation. As commander in chief of the armed forces, he embarked on a program to create a military force capable of the aggression needed for such expansion. In 1935 in violation of the Treaty of Versailles, he ordered a draft of German youth into the army.

In 1936 he again broke the treaty when his troops occupied the Rhineland region of Germany. The treaty had made this a neutral zone, but within its borders were the Krupp armaments factories and the I. G. Farben chemical works, industries necessary to carry out Hitler's further conquests. These conquests followed in quick succession.

German troops moved into Austria in 1938. They were unopposed by the Austrian army, which subsequently pledged allegiance to Hitler. Later that year Hitler's troops occupied the Czechoslovakian territory known as the Sudetenland. In 1939, German soldiers occupied the rest of Czechoslovakia. On September 1, Germany invaded Poland and World War II broke out.

Poland was conquered before the year's end. In 1940, Nazi troops occupied Denmark, Norway, the Netherlands, Belgium, and Luxembourg. They overran France and took Paris. By 1941, British troops had been driven from the European continent. Germany backed up Italy in the invasion of Greece and invaded Yugoslavia. Finally, Hitler broke a pact that had been made with the Soviet Union and attacked Russia. His troops took Kiev, Odessa, and Kharkov, advanced to the outskirts of Leningrad, and continued toward Moscow, causing the Russian government to flee. At this point Hitler's forces were the mightiest war machine the world had ever seen.

"The Final Solution"

Nazi military might was the instrument of Hitler's Aryan policy. The foe were *Untermenschen*, and the Jews of their countries were the lowliest among them. These Jews were at the mercy of Nazi power too often combined with the anti-Semitism of the non-Jewish *Untermenschen* themselves. This combination led to the genocide of the Jews of Europe.

It began in Germany with the roundup of German Jews and their imprisonment in concentration camps. As the German army took over other countries the persecution of Jews continued. In Poland the roundup of Jews and their transfer to ghettos took place during the severe winter of 1939–1940 in forty-degrees-below-zero weather. Babies, children, the ill, and old people died by the thousands from cold and hunger.

In July 1941, Reichmarschall Hermann Göring issued the order for the "final solution of the Jewish question."[5] Killing squads called *Einsatzgruppen* moved into territories the German army had taken and saw to it "that all Jews were . . . exterminated without regard to age or sex."[6] Non-Germans—mostly Ukrainians, Latvians, and Lithuanians—were enlisted to help with the mass executions.

In the beginning this was done mostly by firing squads. The victims were marched off to a secluded area where the shootings might go on all day. But killing people by machine-gun or rifle fire was not efficient enough for the Nazis. The *Einsatzgruppen* next tried killing vans, trucks with sealed compartments, which could hold as many as 150 victims. Carbon monoxide from the vans' exhaust pipes was pumped into the compartments. The killing process took between fifteen and thirty minutes.

However, the process was not always successful, and when it was, there was the problem of what to do with the bodies. Also, the Jews were still not being killed quickly enough to satisfy the Nazis. It was decided to set up permanent camps to handle the problem more efficiently. There would be large chambers in these camps to gas the victims; poisonous Zyklon-B crystals would be used to produce deadly gas; giant ovens would dispose of the bodies. Millions of people, mostly Jews, would die in these death camps.

Righteous Persons

Throughout the years of Nazi rule, their power was absolute, their methods cruel, and vengeance swift. They meted out severe punishment as an example to intimidate those who might think of interfering with their policy of genocide. To oppose them as a Jew meant instant death for oneself and one's loved ones. For non-Jews, to help Jews—even Jewish children—was to risk disaster for oneself, one's family, one's friends, one's village.

To challenge the Nazi genocide policies from a position of neutrality, or even as a German ally, might result in grave consequences at the hands of the government. Clergy who tried to help ended up in concentration camps. Individual helpers might be ostracized by neighbors, and were often betrayed by them.

Yet individuals, clergy, government officials, and even whole villages did help. These people have been honored by the Yad Vashem Holocaust Memorial Museum in Jerusalem as Righteous Persons. As of January 1, 1997, 14,706 people had been so honored. However, Yad Vashem acknowledges that the list is far from complete. Many more unknown individuals risked their lives, and often sacrificed them. This is the story of the heroes of the Holocaust.

Marion Fuerst was a schoolgirl in Stuttgart, Germany, when the Nazis came to power. She was nineteen years old, and World War II had not yet begun when she went to work in a department store as a cashier. It was a time when persecution was making Germany an intolerable place for Jews. They were desperate to leave the country, but the Nazis placed many obstacles in their way. A group of sympathetic Stuttgart businessmen financed a network to help these Jews. They recruited Fuerst to help them.

She was tall, blonde, blue-eyed, and attractive—the very picture of young German womanhood glorified by the Nazis. Her Aryan looks put her beyond suspicion. The network supplied her with forged documents, doctored passports, phony visas, train tickets, and packets of money. Before leaving for work, she would hide these under her clothes, distributing them in different undergarments so that they would not make any lumps, which might be noticed. When a Jewish customer whispered a password—usually a Latin phrase—while paying for a purchase, Fuerst would slip the designated items into the package she was wrapping.

Countless Jews were helped in escaping Germany by Marion Fuerst. What she was doing was against Nazi law. She could have been arrested. She could have gone to prison, most likely to one of the early concentration camps, which had been established in Germany for those who opposed the Nazi regime. She could have been brutalized. She could have ended up dead. But Marion Fuerst was a person of conscience. Taking the risk was quite simply a matter of being true to herself.

Bluffing the Gestapo

The same was true of Countess Maria Helena Francoise Isabel von Maltzan, daughter of a wealthy, titled family with an estate of 18,000 acres (7,285 hectares) in Silesia, Germany. Before the war the countess involved herself in the anti-Nazi resistance while attending the universities of Breslau and Munich. She did this in defiance of her anti-Semitic mother, her field marshal Nazi brother-in-law, and her fanatic Nazi brother. Because of her anti-Nazi activities, her brother later was able to withhold her considerable inheritance from her.

Countess von Maltzan fell in love with a Jewish magazine editor, Hans Hirschel, in Berlin in 1939. When he was threatened with deportation by the Nazis, she hid him in her apartment. Soon the apartment was under surveillance by the Gestapo (Nazi secret police), which had identified the countess as an anti-Nazi and suspected her of being involved in underground activities. In fact, throughout the war, she hid more than sixty Jews in her home at various times.

On one occasion she was taken to Gestapo headquarters for questioning. The countess summoned up the imperial manner of the nobility with whom she had been raised. Sweetly, but haughtily, she asked the Gestapo officer in charge to call a Nazi official close to Hitler and explain why she would not be on time for their luncheon date. The bluff worked and she was released.

The Indomitable Countess

In 1942 the countess became pregnant by Hirschel. A homosexual friend pretended that he was the father of the child. In September the countess entered a

Berlin hospital to have the baby. Shortly after the birth, an air raid cut off the electrical power supply to her infant son's incubator. The child died.

Despite the fact that she was in bad health herself, the countess continued her activities on behalf of Jews. Shortly before the war ended she led a group of refugees through a wooded area to a place on a railway line where an engineer had been bribed to stop a train bound for Sweden. The Jews hid inside crates that were then loaded onto a boxcar of the train. After the train had left, while making her way back, the countess narrowly escaped capture by a Nazi patrol by swimming across a pond. Shivering with cold, she hid in the woods for a day and a half before she was able to make her way home. On a previous occasion she had been less lucky and had received a flesh wound in her neck from a shot by her pursuers.

Why did she do it? "I had read *Mein Kampf*," she said long afterward. "I knew that murders were going on, horrible things were happening, and I would have done anything against it."[1]

Courage and Religion

Throughout the Nazi years there were other Germans like Countess von Maltzan. Most of their names are not known. For those Germans who tried to help Jews, remaining anonymous was often a matter of life or death. When they helped Jews and then parted from them, they would say, "Promise me that you will never tell anyone my name. Don't ever write to me. Good luck."[2]

Likewise, the organization for which Marion Fuerst worked had no name. Its members are still unknown. Nor does anyone really know how many such German organizations, or how many German individuals, helped the Jews throughout the genocide.

Some groups that are known to have helped Jews were religious in nature. One of these was the Confessing Church, a Protestant denomination formed in May 1934, the year after Hitler became chancellor of Germany. One of its goals was to repeal the Nazi law "which required that the civil service would be purged of all those who were either Jewish or of partly Jewish descent." Another was to help those "who suffered through repressive laws, or violence."[3]

About 7,000 of the 17,000 Protestant clergy in Germany joined the Confessing Church. Much of their work has gone unrecognized, but two who will never forget them are Max Krakauer and his wife. Sheltered in sixty-six houses and helped by more than eighty individuals who belonged to the Confessing Church, they owe them their lives.

German Catholic churches went out of their way to protect Catholics of Jewish ancestry. More inclusive was the principled stand taken by Catholic Bishop Clemens Count von Galen of Münster. He publicly denounced the Nazi slaughter of Jews and actually succeeded in having the program halted for a short time. But then it was resumed.

Members of the Society of Friends—German Quakers working with organizations of Friends from other countries—were particularly successful in rescuing Jews. In the early days of Nazi rule they funded Jewish emigration from Germany. When that was no longer possible, they ran a sort of underground railroad, providing refuge, food, and clothing. Some Jews were hidden throughout the war by Quakers in Germany. Jehovah's Witnesses, themselves targeted for concentration camps, also provided help to Jews.

The Martyrdom of Pastor Bonhoeffer

Some of these religious Germans were prominent in their own right. One of these was Pastor Dietrich Bonhoeffer, a founding member of the Confessing Church. From the first days of Hitler he had spoken out against anti-Semitic measures. He challenged Nazi doctrine directly by saying it denied "the explicit teaching and spirit of the Gospel of Jesus Christ."[4] He headed up one of the Confessing Church's seminaries, teaching classes of twenty-plus students that Nazism and anti-Semitism were opposed to their religion.

A pacifist who was opposed to killing, Bonhoeffer was so outraged by Nazi atrocities that he set aside his beliefs to take part in a plot to assassinate Hitler. He acted as a courier between the German generals involved in the plot and representatives of the countries fighting against Germany. The plan was that once Hitler was dead, the generals would negotiate a surrender.

Pastor Bonhoeffer managed a series of trips to Switzerland and Sweden to meet with British and American agents. On one of these trips he carried out a plan known as Operation Seven, which involved smuggling seven Jews from Nazi Germany to Switzerland. When the Nazis found out about Operation Seven, the Jews just barely made their escape and Pastor Bonhoeffer came close to losing his life.

On April 5, 1943, the Gestapo arrested Dietrich Bonhoeffer. It is not clear whether he was arrested for his role in the plot against Hitler or for his involvement in the rescue of fourteen more Jews earlier that month. He was held in various concentration camps until April 9, 1945. On that day, less than a month before the war ended, Pastor Dietrich Bonhoeffer was stripped naked, led to a gallows by Nazi guards, and hanged.

The Scoundrel Hero

The most well-known German hero of the Holocaust, thanks to Steven Spielberg's award-winning film about him, is undoubtedly Oskar Schindler. He was also the most flamboyant. He was a hard-drinking gambler and adulterer, a black marketeer who resorted to bribery, a man who desired money even more than he did the series of women who became his mistresses. He seemed to be a thoroughgoing scoundrel. However, Oskar Schindler had a conscience.

When the German army conquered Poland in 1939, Schindler was right behind them. He cultivated Gestapo bigwigs and through bribery and chicanery persuaded them to turn over to him an enamelware factory formerly owned by Jews. His Gestapo friends even provided Jewish slave laborers for the factory. With a setup like that, it couldn't have been more profitable.

Dietrich Bonhoeffer,
pastor of the
Confessing Church

Schindler, however, could not close his eyes to what was going on all around him. He witnessed roundups of Jewish women and children and watched them being packed into boxcars headed for death camps. He saw Jewish men being lined up and shot down. He witnessed casual brutality on a daily basis. He simply could not stand it. Schindler "resolved to do everything in my power to defeat the [Nazi] system."[5]

He paid off Nazis to have the Jews working in his factory declared essential to the war effort. He insisted the factory required a larger workforce and bribed Nazi officials to get it. He was making money hand over fist, but much of it was going for bribes and to feed his workers adequately. He eventually set up a second factory to manufacture armaments and recruited nine hundred more Jewish workers for it. He added their names to his list of workers essential to the war effort. He allowed them to sabotage the bullets they made. He constantly paid off Nazis and fought off all efforts to remove any Jews from his work sites.

Eventually Schindler spent all of his profits on keeping more than 1,300 Jewish men, women, and children alive. The bribes he paid and the risks he took might easily have landed him in a concentration camp himself. Today he is one of the 311 Germans honored by the Yad Vashem Holocaust Memorial Museum in Jerusalem as Righteous Persons.

The "Petroleum Technicians"

Schindler was not the only German industrialist who risked his life to protect his Jewish workers during the Holocaust years. Berthold Beitz was another. However, in most respects Beitz was very different from Schindler.

Beitz came from a wealthy German family of prominent Nazi supporters. Through his grandfather, young Berthold Beitz was introduced to Reinhard Heydrich, the Gestapo chief and one of the major planners of the genocide of European Jews. This was in 1941, and the Nazis were beginning to take over oil refineries in western Poland. With Heydrich's backing and recommendations from munitions magnates like Alfred Krupp, the twenty-seven-year-old Beitz was appointed director of the Karpaten Oil Company in Borislav, Poland.

Before the war, half the population of Borislav had been Jewish. By the time Beitz arrived, those who weren't dead had been herded into work camps. Beitz had not been there long when he became aware of trains running periodically from Borislav to the death camps of Auschwitz and Treblinka. He watched as frantic mothers and their children, already half starved, were herded like cattle into boxcars so overcrowded that many would die of suffocation before they reached their destination.

The sight appalled Beitz. Feeling he had to do something, he began hiring Jews to work in his refineries in order to save them from the death camps. Lying about their qualifications and experience, he employed manicurists and tailors and cobblers and Jewish religious scholars, issuing documents that described them as "petroleum technicians."[6] He and his young wife took a Jewish child into their home and hid him in defiance of Nazi law decreeing harsh punishment for sheltering Jews.

Sometimes Beitz's workers would be caught in the periodic roundups of Jews. He went frequently to the train station to identify them and to produce documents proving they were essential to the production of petroleum. On one occasion he spied a company secretary and her mother being loaded into a boxcar. He was able to claim the secretary as necessary to his operation, but when the guards insisted the mother must board the train, the daughter insisted on going with her. That was the last Beitz saw of her.

At war's end, Beitz was credited with saving eight hundred Jewish lives. He acted, he says, "out of a sense of humanity."[7]

Political Commitment

Other Germans who helped the Jews from the first days of the Nazis through the end of the war acted from political commitment. In the early days, because they were opponents of the Nazis, groups such as the Social Democrats, Socialists, Communists, trade unionists and other left-wingers were natural allies of the Jews. Later, either out of fear of Nazi power or because German nationalism and anti-Semitism overwhelmed their political commitment, many of them turned their backs on the Jews. But this was not true of all of them.

Although few in number, politically committed anti-Nazis in major cities like Berlin and Frankfurt risked retaliation by hiding whole Jewish families for days, months, years, and through the duration of the war. In rural areas there were German farmers with a tradition of fighting for land reform who took in Jewish children and passed them off as their own. Left-wing resistance fighters helped smuggle Jews out of Germany.

Later in the war, such groups supplied arms to Jews trapped in Eastern Europe. One notable example occurred in the Bialystok ghetto, where Jews were held in appalling conditions before being shipped out to death camps. When they formed into a resistance movement, their biggest problem was acquiring weapons. The solution came voluntarily from Communist and other left-wing German civilians who risked their lives to supply the Jews with guns and ammunition.

One Final Victim

Kurt Gerstein, on the other hand, was far from being a left-winger. He joined the Nazi party in 1933, shortly after Hitler came to power. He believed Nazism would restore Germany's pride in itself. Nevertheless, he had problems as a Nazi. Mainly these came from his inability to take party discipline seriously. He was by nature a practical joker, and he was also rebellious. He was twice arrested for minor offenses and once thrown out of the party. His family had influence, though, and he was allowed to rejoin the Nazi organization.

By the time the war came along, Gerstein was a married man with three children. Trained in both engineering and medicine, he had been assigned by the SS (*Schutzstaffel*—special services personnel who performed mass killings) to the Hygienic Institute. There he devised a delousing procedure for troops in the field and was promoted to lieutenant.

His research activities led to his being sent to Poland in 1942 with a trial quantity of hydrogen cyanide, also known as Zyklon-B. It was supposed to be tested to determine if it was a practical substitute for the gas then being used in the death camps. Gerstein visited the camps of Belzec and Treblinka. He witnessed the murder of Jewish men, women, and children. Horrified, he buried the Zyklon-B without using it.

On the train back to Berlin, by chance Gerstein met the Swedish counsel, Baron Goran von Otter. "Yesterday I saw something horrible," said Gerstein, who went on to describe the murders he had witnessed.[8] He showed von Otter the requisition for the Zyklon-B. He wanted the Swede to contact the British and Americans and ask them to drop millions of leaflets on Germany so that the German people would know what was being done in their name.

Von Otter passed on the message, but the Allies did not act. Gerstein then reported the genocide to a prominent Protestant bishop, Otto Dibelius, and to the Catholic Papal Nuncio, Monsignor Cesare Orsenigo. Nothing came of this either. Risking execution as a traitor, Gerstein then made contact with the Dutch underground. They refused to pass on the story to Allied leaders; they simply didn't believe it.

He continued risking his life in other attempts to reveal the mass murders, but to no avail. His efforts were not only unsuccessful, they were also unrecognized. Sadly and ironically, Kurt Gerstein was arrested by the French as a suspected war criminal after the war ended. He proclaimed his innocence, but he was haunted by his early acceptance of Nazi doctrine and the horror that resulted from it. In July 1945, Kurt Gerstein hanged himself in his jail cell. Many people regard him as one more German victim of the Nazis.

3

COUNTRIES OF CONSCIENCE

BULGARIA

DENMARK

FINLAND

DOMINICAN REPUBLIC

I n Germany in 1933, anti-Nazis used to whisper that "there is one man left in Germany and he is a Bulgarian."[1] The man was Georgi Dimitrov, a Bulgarian Communist accused of setting fire to the Reichstag, the building where the Nazi-controlled German parliament met. During his trial, he proved so strong during a confrontation with number-two Nazi Hermann Göring that he was acquitted. Dimitrov may have been the first Bulgarian to stand up against the Nazis, but he was far from the last.

Bulgaria was an ally of Nazi Germany in World War II. Because Bulgaria was on their side, the Germans turned over to that country territory taken from Yugoslavia and Greece. Despite this, Bulgaria did not cooperate in the genocide of the Jews. According to Holocaust expert Hannah Arendt writing in *Eichmann in Jerusalem,* "not a single Bulgarian Jew" was sent to the death camps or "died an unnatural death" at the hands of the Bulgarians.[2] That may not be literally true, but what is true is that both the Bulgarian government and people resisted Nazi pressure to cooperate in the elimination of Jews to a remarkable extent.

The Yellow Stars

The same cannot be said of many of the countries that fought against the Nazis and were conquered by them. In Poland and the Baltic countries, cooperation was such that 90 percent of Jews there perished. In the Netherlands, 75 percent did not survive. Seventy percent of Hungary's Jews, 65 percent of the Jews of the Ukraine, 60 percent of the Jews of Belgium and Yugoslavia, 50 percent of the Jews of Romania, and 26 percent of the Jews of France were all killed with the collaboration of the governments of those countries and the active cooperation of many of their citizens as well.

The difference in Bulgaria, according to the German ambassador Adolf Beckerle, was that "the Bulgarians had lived for too long with peoples like Armenians, Greeks, and Gypsies to appreciate the Jewish problem."[3] That was his alibi to Berlin explaining why the roundups of Bulgarian Jews for shipment to the death camps was not going as planned. Indeed, even when the Bulgarian government gave in to Nazi anti-Jewish demands, they somehow didn't work out.

Pushed to make Jews wear a yellow star as a badge of shame, the Bulgarian government issued stars so tiny that they were hard to see. Many Jews simply did not wear them. Those who did, according to Nazi Chief of Counterintelligence Walter Schellenberg, received "so many manifestations of sympathy from the misled population that they actually are proud of their sign."[4] It wasn't long before the Bulgarian government did away with the yellow stars altogether.

Proud King Boris

The Nazis wanted to make the capital city of Sofia, Bulgaria, *Judenrein*—free of Jews. The plan was to round up Jews and ship them off to the camps. Instead, the Bulgarian government dispersed the Jews to rural areas where they could not easily be rounded up. The people of Sofia, however, were not happy with this solution. First they went to the railroad station to try to stop the Jews from leaving the city. Then they went to the king's palace and staged a massive protest demonstration.

They were demonstrating for the Jews and against the Nazis, but not against the king. It was well known that Bulgaria's King Boris, like the Bulgarian parliament, did not approve of the Nazis' anti-Semitic policies. Indeed, the

Germans blamed King Boris for shielding the Jews from the death camps. When he was murdered in 1943, there seemed little doubt that Nazi agents had carried out the crime.

Religion also played its part in the Bulgarian resistance to anti-Semitism. The majority of Bulgarians are Eastern Orthodox Christians. The stand of their church during the Nazi years may be judged by the fact that the chief rabbi of Sofia was hidden from the Nazis by Archbishop Stephan of that city. The archbishop said that "men had no right to torture Jews, and to persecute them."[5]

The Stand-Up Finns

Another ally of Germany that balked at persecuting Jews was Finland. In 1939 and 1940, Finland had fought a war against the Soviet Union and lost territory to the Russians. There were only 2,000 Jews in Finland at that time, but they were extremely patriotic and answered the call to arms. Twenty-three of them died fighting the Russians. In recognition of their loyalty and courage, the Finnish commander in chief, Field Marshal Carl Gustaf von Mannerheim, went to the Helsinki synagogue and presented the Jewish community with a wreath in their memory.

When Germany invaded Russia in June 1941, Finland also declared war on Russia. Finland wanted its territory back. Germany wanted to keep Russian warships and allied merchant ships out of the Baltic Sea. Control of the Gulf of Finland was crucial to that aim.

It was important to the Germans not to alienate the Finns, but that didn't stop the Nazis from trying to persuade them to make Finland *Judenrein*. In July 1942, SS Chief Heinrich Himmler went to Helsinki to enlist government cooperation in deporting Finland's Jews to the concentration camps he controlled. Finnish Foreign Minister Rolf Witting refused even to discuss the matter. Commander in chief Mannerheim was more direct. He informed the Germans that if even one of his country's 2,000 Jews was touched, Finland would declare war on Germany. Not one Finnish Jew died in the Holocaust.

King Boris of Bulgaria (left) greets Adolf Hitler on a visit to Germany. The king would later be murdered, presumably because of his opposition to the Nazis' anti-Semitic policies.

The Dominican Welcome Mat

Finland was on Germany's side in World War II, but few of the nations that fought against the Nazis were as concerned about the Jews as the Finns were. Before the war Jewish refugees were turned away by the United States, Britain, Australia, Cuba, and some South American countries, to name a few. A notable exception was the Dominican Republic.

In 1938, Generalissimo Rafael Trujillo, dictator of the Dominican Republic, offered to give sanctuary to 100,000 endangered Jews. However, escape from Europe became almost impossible for Jews after the war started. Only 5,000 Dominican visas were issued to Jews between 1940 and 1945, and only 645 European Jews—mostly from Germany and Austria—were actually able to make their way to the Dominican Republic.

Despite the fact that the Dominican Republic is a very poor country, the Jews were welcomed with open arms. They were settled in the tiny seacoast town of Sousa, an overgrown area that had been cleared for farming thanks to funding provided by the American Jewish Joint Distribution Committee. Each new arrival was given 80 acres (32 hectares) of land, ten cows, a mule, and a horse by the Dominican government. The Jews established a farming cooperative—*Productos Sousa*—that, to this day, still produces much of the Dominican Republic's meat and dairy products. They have established a museum to keep alive the record of how one small island nation in the Caribbean set a humanitarian example when so many other countries turned their backs.

The King's Yellow Star

One of the most stirring examples of decency and courage in the face of Nazi anti-Semitism is the record of Denmark. On April 9, 1940, Germany invaded neutral Denmark and occupied the capital city of Copenhagen. The Nazis tried to institute their usual anti-Semitic measures.

As in other conquered countries, they issued an edict that Jews must wear a yellow badge with a star on it. Immediately, King Christian X announced that he would be the first to wear the badge. Other representatives of the Danish government informed the Nazis that all Danish government officials would resign before they would enforce anti-Jewish measures.

The Nazis offered a compromise. There were 8,000 Jews in Denmark, but only 6,500 of them were Danish citizens. The rest were refugees who had fled to Denmark from other countries the Nazis had taken over. If the Danes would identify these non-Danish Jews, the Nazis would be glad to take them off their hands. Again the Danish government refused to cooperate.

This was the situation until 1943 when Hitler decided to incorporate the nation of Denmark into Germany. When the Danes learned of his intention, their resistance stiffened, and sabotage of German military installations increased. Then, in May 1943, Nazi Police Battalion 65 was sent to Copenhagen.

"An Extraordinary Operation"

Police Battalion 65 was fresh from Poland, where they had carried out mass executions of Jewish men, women, and children. They were possibly the most efficient weapon in the Nazi arsenal when it came to rounding up and killing Jews. But in Poland they had found members of the local population to cooperate with them, by pointing out Jews and even helping with the killings. Denmark was a different story. The Danish population would not betray the Jews.

Frustrated at almost every turn, Police Battalion 65 left Denmark in February 1944. During the time they were there, they had been a key part of one of the great Nazi failures of the Holocaust. Denmark had been put under martial law by the Germans, and the Nazis had scheduled a roundup of the Jews for October 1, 1943. Three days before that date, on September 28, Danish Social Democratic party leaders learned of the plan and informed the government.

What followed, as described by Holocaust historian Lucy S. Dawidowicz, was "an extraordinary operation involving the whole Danish people and the agreement of the Swedish government."[6] As far as the Germans were concerned, by October 1 it appeared as if the Jews of Denmark had vanished. Actually, the Danes were hiding them. Over the next month Danish fishing boats smuggled 5,919 Jews across the straits to neutral Sweden.

The remainder of the Jews were hidden by the Danes in Denmark. Some four hundred of them were rounded up by Police Battalion 65 and shipped to Theresienstadt concentration camp. The Danish government immediately lodged an international protest and demanded to inspect the camp. The Danish Red Cross made repeated visits to Theresienstadt after June 1944. They were so persistent that despite the fact that Theresienstadt was usually only a way station on the road to the gas ovens of Auschwitz, none of the Jews from Denmark were sent to their death.

The only Danish Jews who died during the Holocaust died of old age. When we speak of a truly humane country, surely Denmark must head the list.

olf and Esther Fullenbaum and their four-year-old daughter, Carlotta, were Jewish refugees who, like many others, fled from Germany to Italy. In comparison to other European countries, there was very little history of anti-Semitism in Italy. Although it was a Fascist country ruled by dictator Benito Mussolini, Italy had refused to deport Jews to the death camps. It was only after the Germans occupied Italy to fight Allied invasion troops in November 1943 that such deportations of Jews occurred. By then the Fullenbaum family had relocated in the central Italian town of Secchiano.

A "Conspiracy of Goodness"

What followed has been called a "conspiracy of goodness."[1] The conspiracy involved the entire population of Secchiano—six hundred citizens. For more than a year the villagers hid the Fullenbaums during a series of raids by Nazi soldiers. While hiding and unable to work, the Fullenbaums' money ran out. The townspeople fed, clothed, and housed the family. When the Nazis arrested the village priest for harboring other Jewish fugitives and deported him to a concentration camp, the people of Secchiano still stood by the Fullenbaums.

"Their presence was a matter of public knowledge and private pride," according to Holocaust scholar Eva Fogelman.[2] When Nazi soldiers began house-to-house searches, the Fullenbaums were taken from their hiding place on the second floor of the schoolhouse and brought out to the fields to be passed off as farmworkers. When the soldiers rounding up Jews came to the fields to interrogate the workers, they were told that the Fullenbaums were deaf-mutes. That kept the Jewish family's German accents from giving them away. Eventually, the villagers of Secchiano helped the Fullenbaums escape to British-held territory.

Sanctuary in Assisi

The people of Secchiano acted at grave risk to themselves. The Nazis frequently shot and killed those who hid Jews, or publicly hanged them as an example. It was a carrot-and-stick approach in which they offered a reward to those who turned in Jews. The bounty might be a carton of cigarettes, a few pounds of sugar, a bottle of liquor, or even some money. In many countries of Europe, people were all too eager to accept such payment for betraying Jews. In Italy, however, such betrayals were rare.

Some Italians who organized to save Jews acted out of religious conviction. This often meant defying the highest authority of their church. In 1933 the Vatican Concordat had been signed between Hitler and the Roman Catholic Church. It was an agreement that the Church would not meddle in affairs of state and that the Nazis would leave the Church alone. Nevertheless, on local levels many Italian Catholic clergy did organize to impede the carrying out of Nazi *Judenrein* policies.

The Franciscan monks of Assisi, for instance, decided that the Catholic tradition of sanctuary applied to Jews. Giuseppe Placido Nicolini, bishop of Assisi, found refuge among members of Assisi congregations for hundreds of Jews. With Don Aldo Brunacci, a canon of the San Rufino Cathedral, he set up a network to provide identification papers for Jews that would establish them as Catholics. Many of the refugees were hidden in the Convent of the Stigmata.

They were served kosher meals. A school was set up for Jewish children to study their own religion. No attempt was made to convert them to Catholicism.

In 1944, Father Brunacci was arrested for shielding Jews from Nazi authorities. Only a plea on his behalf from the Vatican saved him from execution. He was exiled from Assisi. All of the Jews he had helped shelter there, however, survived the Holocaust.

Father Brunacci's arrest came the year after the Italian army's surrender to American and British troops had left the half of Italy not yet reached by them under German military control. On September 24, 1943, Herbert Kappler, the SS boss in Rome, had received orders to round up all Italian Jews and ship them to Germany. The German ambassador to Rome, whose Italian mistress was hiding a family of Jews in her basement, refused to cooperate with Kappler. Nor would German Field Marshal Kesserling, who claimed he needed the Jews to build fortifications against the advancing armies, cooperate. Nevertheless, Kappler blackmailed Rome's Jewish community, demanding 50 kilograms (110 pounds) of gold within thirty-six hours and threatening to kill two hundred Jews if the gold was not delivered. The gold was obtained from many non-Jews, including parish priests. Even Pope Pius XII offered to provide gold, but by the time he made the offer, the amount needed had already been secured.

When Kappler's SS superiors learned what he had done, they sent forty-four SS killers under Theodor Dannecker to round up Jews in Rome. The German ambassador warned the Pope, who instructed priests to give the Jews sanctuary. The Vatican took in 477 Jews, and an additional 4,238 were hidden in convents and monasteries.

The Catholic Rescuers

In other countries, which did not have Italy's tradition of tolerance toward Jews, the Catholic Church often stood as a bulwark against Nazi anti-Semitism. The Church in the Netherlands condemned the Dutch Nazi movement. It strongly opposed Catholics joining the Nazis. Later, during the German occupation, the leadership of the Church prohibited Dutch Catholic policemen from participating in the Nazi roundups of Jews. The prohibition specified that they could not do so even if it meant being fired from their jobs.

Rescue efforts by the Catholic Church in Poland stemmed from the firm stand against persecuting Jews by Count Andreas Szeptycki, the archbishop of Lvov. He ordered that all priests reporting to him take whatever measures were necessary to save Jewish lives. These measures were sometimes organized by the mother superiors of convents. This was particularly dangerous because Catholic nuns were themselves persecuted after the invasion of Poland. This persecution came from both the Nazis and the Russians who occupied eastern Poland. Nevertheless, in German-occupied Poland the nuns in 189 convents saved the lives of more than 1,500 Jewish children by hiding and caring for them throughout the war.

The Catholic clergy in Belgium also coordinated efforts to rescue Jews. The hierarchy of the Belgian Catholic Church was vocal in its support of these efforts. Cardinal van Roey, backed by Belgium's Queen Mother, Elisabeth, persuaded the Nazis to exempt Belgian Jews from deportation. This agreement was eventually broken by the Nazis, and about a thousand Belgian Jews, along with thousands of other Jews who had sought refuge in Belgium, were sent to the death camps. Nevertheless, the Belgian Catholic Church did try to save Jewish lives.

So too did the Church in France. When France surrendered to Germany in 1940, the country was split in two. One part was ruled directly by the German Nazis. The other—known as Vichy—was ruled by a French pro-Nazi puppet government that essentially took its orders from Berlin. In both areas there were roundups of Jews. In both areas the leaders of the Catholic Church spoke out against the roundups and against the brutal treatment of Jews. At the same time, priests and nuns were creating networks to move Jews around from monasteries to parish houses to private homes in order to keep them out of Nazi hands.

The Heroes of Le Chambon-sur-Lignon

It was not just French Catholics who opposed the Holocaust. In Vichy it was Protestant leader Marc Boegner who defied the government with public statements denouncing anti-Jewish measures. In particular, it was the Protestant clergy of the French village of Le Chambon-sur-Lignon that coordinated one of the most remarkable rescue operations of the war.

Five thousand inhabitants of Le Chambon were involved. Most of them were descendants of Huguenots who had survived the persecution and massacres of the sixteenth century. However, about 20 percent of the villagers were Catholics. The difference in religion didn't matter. All of the villagers cooperated in saving the Jews from the Nazis.

Le Chambon was a resort village, located high in the mountains where the air is pure. During the war, injured or ill German soldiers were sent there to convalesce. Because it was situated on a main travel route, many Jews fleeing Vichy roundups also arrived in Le Chambon. As this became known, both Vichy and German soldiers periodically raided the town to search for Jews.

The people of Le Chambon stubbornly refused to cooperate with such efforts. They made no secret of their opposition to the anti-Semitic policies of the Nazis and their puppets. Schoolchildren refused to salute the Vichy flag when it was raised each morning. When the Vichy minister for youth affairs visited Le Chambon, he was handed a pledge signed by high-school students. It promised that "if our comrades, whose only fault is to be born in another religion, receive the order to let themselves be deported, or even examined, they will disobey the orders received, and we will try to hide them as best we can."[3]

The Ever-Present Danger

Eleven pastors were involved in the ongoing Le Chambon rescue operations. The leading figure among them was Pastor Andre Trocme. When a Vichy official told him that foreign Jews—refugees—"are not your brothers," Pastor Trocme replied that "we do not know what Jews are. We only know men."[4]

A group of Jewish girls poses with Dr. Juliette Usach (in glasses), one of the many residents of Le Chambon-sur-Lignon who shielded fleeing Jews from Nazi roundups.

The "men"—and the women and children—who fled to Le Chambon would check into one of the resort hotels as guests. After one night there, Pastor Trocme and the other pastors saw to it that they were dispersed among local homes and farms. Here they were hidden until the danger of discovery by Vichy Nazi raiding parties became so great that they were passed along to another hiding place. In this fashion, the people of Le Chambon saved between 2,500 and 5,000 Jews.

"No one knew what the consequences of hiding Jews might be," remembers Lesley Maber, an English teacher who lived in Le Chambon. "The sense of danger was always present, but we never spoke of it."

Nevertheless, it was quite real. Daniel Trocme, a schoolteacher nephew of the pastor Andre Trocme, ran a boarding school for Jewish children. One day he and three busloads of children were seized by the Gestapo. The teacher and his students went to their deaths in the gas chambers of the Majdanek concentration camp.

Pastor Trocme himself, along with two other clergymen, spent a month in a Vichy prison camp. They were told they would be freed if they signed a loyalty oath to the Vichy regime. They refused to sign. Later they were released anyway, possibly because of pressure brought by other members of the clergy.

A tribute to the people of Le Chambon comes from Andre Chouraqui, an Algerian Jew who worked with an organization dedicated to saving Jewish children. His job was to find hiding places for them in the mountains around Le Chambon. On one occasion he was tipped off by a local resident that the Gestapo was looking for him. The warning saved his life. "Not a single time while I was there did the Christians refuse to help us in every way possible," he testifies.[5] It is a sentiment echoed by many Jews who owed the people of Le Chambon their lives.

The "Angel of Lvov"

There was no history of anti-Semitism in Le Chambon. In Lvov, Poland, it was different. As in other parts of Poland, over the years there had been periodic pogroms against the Jews. Nevertheless, there were brave and humane Poles in Lvov who acted to protect the Jews from the Nazis. The city's union of sanitation workers hid Jews in the city sewers. They brought them food and moved them around to avoid periodic inspections by the Nazis. They even arranged to have sympathetic doctors brought down into the sewers to treat the sick.

Another group was organized to help Jews in Lvov by Wladislawa Choms, the wife of a Polish army officer. She had spoken out against Polish anti-Semitism as early as 1937. In June 1941, when the Nazis entered Lvov, her husband was arrested. Nevertheless, Mrs. Choms enlisted a group of Poles to find hiding places for Jews. They provided forged papers for Jews—particularly children—who could pass for Christian Poles. They collected gold and jewels from wealthy Jews and used the money they raised to help poorer Jews. Mrs. Choms succeeded in placing many Jewish children in orphanages and monasteries. Sixty Polish families were recruited by her organization to take in Jewish babies and pass them off as their own.

Eventually Mrs. Choms had to flee the Germans. She went to Warsaw and stayed there until the end of the war. Many years later she went to Jerusalem to be honored at Yad Vashem. She was known, remembered one of those she had saved, as the "Angel of Lvov."[6]

Zegota

Groups like those organized by Mrs. Choms in Lvov were in contrast to the many Poles who either stood by passively while the Jews were rounded up or actively cooperated in their genocide. These rescuers must be a source of pride to the Poles. The most effective of them was a network called Zegota.

The code name Zegota stood for *Rada Pomocy Zydom*, which translates as Council for Aid to Jews. Zegota "was run jointly by Jews and non-Jews from a wide range of political movements."[7] The little money that was provided for its operations came from the Polish government-in-exile in London. It was used to feed, clothe, hide, and transport Jews to safety.

Zegota operated underground in Poland between December 1942 and January 1945, the period of the so-called Final Solution during which the Nazis stepped up exterminations to kill millions of additional Jews. For trying to help these Jews, Zegota members faced death. Indeed, the founder of the organization, Catholic writer Zifia Kossak-Szczucka, died at Auschwitz. Another rescuer survived, but at a price.

Her name was Barbara Makuch. She was a young Polish woman who followed in the footsteps of two of her relatives when they joined Zegota. After carrying out several missions successfully, she was caught by the Gestapo with packages containing foreign money and forged documents. They wanted her to betray the other members of her organization. She refused. Barbara Makuch was tortured, whipped, and repeatedly beaten. She lost all her teeth. When she still refused to name names, she was sent to Ravensbruck concentration camp. Somehow she survived there until the end of the war when the camp was liberated by the American army. Like Wladislawa Choms, Barbara Makuch has been honored by Yad Vashem.

The Emergency Rescue Committee

One of the few United States citizens celebrated by Yad Vashem was Varian Fry. He worked for a group called the Emergency Rescue Committee, which had been formed in New York City in 1940, around the time that France surrendered to Germany. At that time many European Jews had fled from their native countries to France. Now they were fleeing from German-occupied France to Vichy, unaware that while the regime there was French, its armistice with the Germans required it to turn over non-French Jews to the Nazis. The Emergency Rescue Committee learned of this. It also learned of a secret Gestapo list containing the names of well-known Jewish and non-Jewish writers, philosophers, artists, economists, and others who had criticized the Nazis publicly. These notables were viewed as especially at risk, and the committee's goal was to keep them out of Nazi hands.

The committee approached the United States State Department to ask that the strict limits on refugee immigration be relaxed. They got nowhere. They then directed their plea to the president's wife, Eleanor Roosevelt. Possibly due to her intervention, President Roosevelt ordered that emergency visas be issued.

That was only the first step. The endangered refugees still had to be located. The visas had to be gotten to them. They had to be helped to elude the Nazis and make their way to consulates (foreign government offices) where the visas would be honored. All this required an organization with a variety of contacts and skills. Somebody had to set up this organization. Varian Fry volunteered, and the committee accepted him for the job.

Varian Fry

Varian Fry was a thirty-two-year-old writer and editor who was fluent in several languages. Explaining his decision to volunteer, he said that "among the refugees caught in France were many writers and artists whose work I had enjoyed. . . . Now that they were in danger, I felt obliged to help them if I could; just as they, without knowing it, had often in the past helped me."[8]

Helping wasn't easy. The United States had not yet entered the war, but Americans were regarded with suspicion by the Nazis and their puppets. Nevertheless, Fry decided to go to the French seaport of Marseilles. Many refugees had fled there after the Germans occupied Paris. Boats sailed from there, and many railroad lines intersected there. Also, it was not far from the border of Spain, which was a neutral country.

Soon it was being whispered among the refugees in Marseilles that there was an American with U. S. visas who had come to help them escape Vichy France. Fry was besieged with pleas for help. He quickly realized that he couldn't handle this all by himself and—with great care—he began enlisting others to help him. He found his way into the black market of Marseilles, and from there into certain very useful sectors of the underworld. With money from the committee, he hired a full-time expert forger. He made contact with bandits who supplied maps of little-known routes through the mountains to the Spanish border. He learned which officials could be bribed.

Among the staff he assembled were several young Americans who had been stranded in Europe by the war. There were also artists from a variety of European countries who could alter photographs for documents. There were natives of Marseilles who could move around more freely than the Americans and non-French Europeans. They served as couriers and set up meetings with corrupt officials.

Defying the Authorities

The American consular officials in Marseilles refused to honor the visas Fry had brought with him unless those using them had obtained exit permits from the French. Also, if flight was to take the refugees through such countries as Spain, Portugal, Turkey, or others, transit visas were required from the consular offices of those countries. Only a limited number of ships' captains could be bribed to overlook the lack of some of this paperwork. Escape by railroad was more difficult because many borders might have to be crossed, and this meant that many border guards and train conductors would have to be bribed. There was no telling who might turn in a refugee with questionable papers.

Fry and his associates escorted many younger refugees over the escape routes through the Pyrenees Mountains to Spain. Older refugees, however, couldn't make the climb. Fry rented a villa outside Marseilles, moved into it, and hid refugees there. The surrealist poet Andre Breton and his family took refuge in the villa, as did many surrealist artists who were on the Gestapo's special hit list because the Nazis considered the strange, dreamlike surrealist art to be evidence of *Untermenschen* depravity.

Fortunately for the Breton family, they had left by the time Vichy police descended on the villa. Varian Fry and other members of his organization were imprisoned on a prison ship in the harbor of Marseilles. Fry, being an American citizen, made the Vichy government nervous, and he was released several days after his arrest. By then his American passport had run out. The State Department, leery of his activities, refused to renew it. Fry stayed anyway, continuing to run his organization of rescuers and taking his chances.

He remained in the Marseilles area for a year before the Vichy French finally threw him out of the country. By then he and his colleagues had successfully helped 1,500 people escape Vichy France and the Nazis. They had also given help and support to 2,500 others. In 1967 he was honored by France, the country that had expelled him, with the *Croix de Chevalier*—a medal of the French Legion of Honor. It is also worth noting that today the Emergency Rescue Committee, now known as the International Rescue Committee, provides aid to refugees all over the world.

5

THE HEROIC IMPULSE

onsidering the number of people slaughtered by the Nazis and their collaborators, it's easy to conclude that the Holocaust brought out the worst in people. It's less easy to appreciate that it brought out the best in a great many other people. These were men and women from many countries and from every walk of life who risked their own safety, and sometimes the safety of their loved ones, to save Jews from genocide.

Some, as we have seen, were members of groups organized to fight this genocide. Others, however, acted as individuals, responding to their own conscience, behaving with courage because the dangers involved were easier to live with than the shame of averting their eyes. Among these individuals were generals, civil servants, housewives, doctors, social workers, and many others.

The names of most of these rescuers are unremembered or unknown. Many died at the hands of the Nazis with no recognition of the good they had done, or attempted to do. Among the few who are remembered and honored is Jan Karski, a Pole who risked his life behind Nazi lines to bring back evidence of the slaughter of Jews to the leaders of Western nations.

Linked to the Downtrodden

Ten years before the war, when Jan Karski was fifteen years old, he received a bicycle and some money from his grandmother and was told to travel around his country in order to see how different kinds of people lived. His journey took him to eastern Poland where he saw Ukrainian and Byelorussian peasants living in thatch huts along with their animals. The land didn't belong to them, but they worked it from dawn to dusk. They were sad and weary and often hopeless people. Young Karski had never seen such poverty, and he was shocked by it. At the same time, he realized that because they were human beings and he was a human being, he was linked to them. It was the birth of a lifelong conviction that he was personally linked to the downtrodden and persecuted of the world.

In 1939, while serving in the Polish army, Karski was taken prisoner by the Russians who invaded Poland from the east in cooperation with the German invasion from the west. He escaped the Russians, made contact with Polish resistance groups, and began his dangerous career as a courier between them. When the Germans caught him, he tried to commit suicide rather than give away his comrades. He survived the attempt, and an underground raiding party rescued him.

For the next two years he continually risked his life to crisscross Nazi lines. He was the contact person between the Polish government-in-exile in London and various partisan groups. This role took Karski to Warsaw in 1942. Here non-Jewish Polish resistance fighters put him in contact with Jewish underground leaders in the Warsaw ghetto.

The Failed Mission

Conditions in the Warsaw ghetto—children and old people freezing to death, dying of starvation and disease—were appalling. Even more shocking were the stories Jewish resistance leaders told Karski of trainloads of Warsaw Jews being shipped to death camps. He found it hard to believe such massacres were occurring. He decided to see for himself.

Disguised in the uniform of a Latvian auxiliary policeman, Karski visited two death camps, Treblinka and Bergen-Belsen. He saw freight cars packed so densely with Jews that when they were unloaded, a large percentage of those inside were corpses. He saw Jews gassed in railway trucks. He did not personally see Jews going to their death in the new gas chambers, but he knew from many sources that this was happening.

By the time Karski made his way back to London, he was determined to do everything he could to stop the Holocaust. He passed on requests from the Jewish resistance leaders to the Polish government-in-exile in London that the trains carrying Jews to the camps be bombed. However, the bombing of troop and munition trains had priority, and that wasn't done. From November 1942 through July 1943, Karski pleaded with the highest officials of every Allied government to act to stop the genocide of Europe's Jews. On July 28, Karski personally met with President Franklin D. Roosevelt to plead with him to take action to rescue the Jews.

His mission failed. He kept trying until the end of the war, but with no success. To Jan Karski, as he said many years later, "all murdered Jews became my family."[1]

A Polish Heroine

Jan Karski reported during the war that women were better suited for rescue work and resistance than men. He found them more sensitive to danger, less apt to take foolish chances, and more committed to success. He praised them as liaison workers and couriers, and as lookouts. He said they were particularly adept at moving refugees from safe house to safe house. The main concern of many of these women was securing safe havens for Jewish children.

A countrywoman of Karski's, social worker Irena Sendlerowa of Warsaw, was one such woman. When the war started she was working in the social-welfare department of the municipal administration of Warsaw. After the Germans sealed off the Jews in the Warsaw ghetto, Sendlerowa used the records of the department to set up a secret welfare network to provide food, medicine, clothing, and sometimes forged documents to Jews. Under her direction, 2,500

Irena Sendlerowa as a girl

Jewish children were sneaked out of the ghetto and hidden with non-Jewish Poles in what was then Christian Warsaw.

Sendlerowa worked with five Jewish youth leaders who themselves declined to escape so that they might help younger children to safety. One of them, Rachela, had a pass to work outside the ghetto. When she went to work, she would take children out with her, explaining that they were younger brothers or sisters, and that there was no one at home to take care of them while she worked. One day a Christian friend warned her that she was being watched and that if she again returned to the ghetto without the children she had taken out, the Gestapo would seize her. She ignored the warning, and the Nazis killed her.

In 1943, Sendlerowa herself was arrested by the Gestapo. She was tortured in an effort to gain the names of her accomplices, and when she continued to refuse to supply the information, she was sentenced to death. Members of Zegota bribed a guard to free her at the last minute and to hand in a report that she had been executed. Despite her narrow escape, Sendlerowa continued working from her hiding place to save Jewish children until the end of the war.

"Yvonne's Children"

Like Irena Sendlerowa, another administrative social worker, Yvonne Nevejean of Belgium, defied the anti-Semitic laws under the Nazi occupation. Director of *l'Oeuvre National de l'Enfance*, the Belgian organization for child welfare, Nevejean acted completely on her own to save Jewish children. She didn't seek authorization, and she didn't consult with her superiors. She worked with a Jewish defense committee to make contact with the children. She supplied them with false identity cards and food-ration coupons. She arranged for the children to be transported to safe houses, convents, or boarding schools. Some of them remained in these places. Others were placed in foster homes. She arranged for messages to be passed between the children and their parents, but the parents weren't told where the children had been taken. This was in order to protect those who gave them refuge.

When the Gestapo seized fifty-eight Jewish children in October 1942, Nevejean went to Queen Mother Elisabeth of Belgium to plead for them. The queen mother interceded with the German general in command. The children were spared.

On another occasion the Gestapo forced Nevejean to accompany them to an orphanage so that they might separate the Jewish children. She arranged matters so that the agents had to report to their superiors that there were no Jewish children to be found. Actually, more than a third of the children in the orphanage were Jews placed there by Nevejean.

Thanks to her efforts, more than three thousand Belgian Jewish children survived the Holocaust at a time when more than one out of three of Belgium's Jews perished. The children became known as "Yvonne's children." When she was honored in Israel in 1965, Yvonne Nevejean said she had acted "simply out of love for those who were suffering the most horribly during the German occupation."[2]

Courage in the Netherlands

Yvonne Nevejean had also acted at great risk to herself. Under the Nazis, there was danger everywhere. In Amsterdam, the Netherlands, a sixteen-year-old girl greeted a man she knew who had been arrested by German soldiers as a partisan. They immediately arrested her as well. Soon after, she was sent to a concentration camp. She hadn't been there long when she was killed for talking back to a guard.

Amsterdam was also the city where Miep Gies and her husband hid teenager Anne Frank (author of a diary that would characterize the Holocaust for millions of readers), her family, and others. Gies had to buy food for nine people, including the seven Jews she was hiding. When the man from whom she bought vegetables noticed the large amounts she was buying, he said nothing. He simply put aside enough to fill her needs. One day Gies arrived to find the store boarded up and the man gone. He had been arrested for hiding two Jews.

Miep Gies originally came from Vienna. She went to Amsterdam as a child, one of many sent by an international program organized to feed undernourished children. The kindness she received from the family who took her in was the basis of her kindness in helping the Frank family. Her efforts were in vain. The Frank family was betrayed, and all but Anne's father died in the death camps. Despite this tragedy, Gies thought that there is goodness in most people. She estimated that she was only one of 20,000 people in the Netherlands who sheltered Jews from the Nazis.

Muslim Rescuers

Often, those who helped the persecuted set aside other loyalties to do so. Before and during World War II the Muslim minority in what was then Yugoslavia was sometimes persecuted by the Serbs. When the Nazis invaded Yugoslavia, the Serbs fought them while many Muslims, like many Croats, collaborated with the Germans.

There were, however, exceptions. One Muslim family who hid Jews during the Holocaust was rescued from the ethnic cleansing that took place in Kosovo in the mid-1990s and brought to Israel and safety by descendants of those they had helped in World War II. Another Yugoslavian Muslim was brought to Israel earlier when those she had helped arranged for her to be honored.

Her name was Zaneiba Hardaga. She had saved two Jewish families from the Nazis. The Germans had executed her devoutly Muslim father for hiding a third Jewish family. Asked why she and her father had put their lives in danger, Zaneiba Hardaga's answer was simple: "Humanity does not know fear," she said.[3]

"The Honor of the Italian Army"

Equally fearless were high-ranking Italian generals who refused to carry out orders to turn over Jews and other refugees to the Nazis. In Yugoslavia, General Mario Roatta, General Mario Robotti, and other commanders granted asylum to the Jews in the areas their armies controlled. In Italian-occupied France, General Vittorio Ambrosio and his officers repeatedly thwarted Nazi efforts to deport the thousands of Jews who had fled to the zone they occupied.

Before Mussolini's anti-Semitic edicts, there had always been high-ranking Jewish officers in the Italian army. They had earned the respect of their non-Jewish comrades in World War I and other conflicts. There simply was not much anti-Semitism in the Italian army.

Certainly General Paride Negri had none. He reacted with fury when a German general, his superior, ordered that he turn over the Jews in his charge to be shipped to concentration camps. "Oh, no," General Negri told him. "That is totally impossible because the deportation of Jews goes against the honor of the Italian army."[4]

THREE VALIANT CONSULS

6

During wartime, the only foreign consular offices in Nazi-controlled countries were either those of German allies or those of neutral nations. They were subject to diplomatic pressures and required to obey the laws laid down by the Nazis. Nevertheless, there were some diplomats who deliberately set out to disobey those laws in order to save Jews from Nazi genocide. These individuals risked their careers, and sometimes their lives. They are not to be forgotten.

Raoul Wallenberg's "Swedish Houses"

The most famous, and possibly the most successful, diplomat to thwart Nazi genocide was Raoul Wallenberg. In June 1944 the thirty-two-year-old Wallenberg was appointed first secretary of the Swedish legation in Budapest, the capital city of Hungary. Before accepting the position, he had insisted upon and received permission from the Swedish government to take whatever actions he deemed necessary to rescue Jews from the Nazis.

By this time more than 400,000 Hungarian Jews had been deported to concentration camps. There were about 230,000 Jews left in Budapest, and the German SS officer in charge of deportations, the infamous Adolf Eichmann, was already arranging for death trains for them. He was temporarily delayed when diplomatic pressure was put on the Hungarian government by King Gustav V of Sweden.

Meanwhile, Wallenberg was distributing bribes and blackmailing officials in order to set up a system for keeping Jews out of Nazi hands. He had safe passes printed in blue and yellow with the coat of arms of the Three Crowns of Sweden on them along with many official-looking stamps and signatures. They were meaningless, but both the Germans and Hungarians were so respectful of authority that many Jews were able to move around by flashing them at checkpoints. Wallenberg handed out more than 13,000 of these passes.

He built thirty safe houses for Jews. He had Swedish flags hung in front of their doors and declared that they were extensions of the Swedish consulate and therefore Swedish territory. Some 15,000 Jews were sheltered in them. The Hungarians called them "Swedish houses."

Thwarting Adolf Eichmann

Toward the end of the war the Hungarian Nazi government declared that Wallenberg's passes were invalid and should not be honored. By this time Wallenberg had made a friend of the Baroness Elizabeth "Liesel" Kemeny, the wife of the Hungarian foreign minister. Through her influence, Wallenberg's passes were once again made valid.

Now Adolf Eichmann, faced with a shortage of railroad cars to transport Jews to extermination camps, started brutal death marches from Budapest to the Austrian border. Many Jews died of starvation and exposure to the cold. Others who couldn't keep up were shot by their Nazi guards. The march was 125 miles (200 kilometers), and periodically Raoul Wallenberg would drive up to the line of prisoners to hand out food and medicine. He also handed out his Swedish passes. Then he would bribe and threaten the guards until those with the passes were released to him.

When Eichmann started loading Budapest's remaining Jews into boxcars bound for the gas chambers, Wallenberg rushed to the railroad station. He climbed on the boxcar roofs, and ran alongside the tracks, maneuvering ceaselessly to hand out bunches of Swedish passes to those inside the cars. The Nazi guards fired on him. Undaunted, Wallenberg turned on them and demanded that those in the boxcars with Swedish passes be released.

Sometimes the guards were intimidated by his authoritarian manner and did release the Jews with passes. Sometimes, this being near the end of the war with confusion everywhere, the passes were honored when they were produced at the train's destination. Sometimes, however, the victims were still holding Swedish passes when they were marched into the gas chambers.

As the war ended, Raoul Wallenberg was taken into custody by the Russians who captured Budapest. It has never been clear why he was arrested or what was done with him. He was never heard from again. But his name lives on in the history of the 97,000 Budapest Jews who survived the Holocaust.

All Jews Are Spanish

Another diplomat in Budapest during the war who set out to help the Jews was a Spaniard, Angel Sanz Briz. Eventually, since they were both dedicated to the same cause, he worked for a time with Raoul Wallenberg. Mostly, however, he acted on his own.

In 1944, appalled at what his wife said he called "the collective madness that came over the Nazis," he nevertheless proceeded diplomatically.[1] He called on a *Gauleiter* (Nazi area commander) to protest the treatment of the Jews. The *Gauleiter* responded angrily that all foreign diplomats cared about was the Jews, never about the Hungarians being starved and beaten during the ferocious campaign being waged by the Russians as they invaded Hungary in pursuit of the retreating Nazi armies.

Sanz Briz was sympathetic. He sent the *Gauleiter* money to help the Hungarian refugees. Thankful, the officer issued an order that the military should respect all buildings under Spanish sovereignty. Sans Briz also secured permission from the Hungarian government to transfer two hundred Jews of Spanish origin to Spain. The two hundred Jews became two hundred families, and periodically the number was mysteriously increased. Sans Briz adopted the attitude that all the Jews in Budapest must be of Spanish origin.

He rented nine buildings where "we housed as many Jews as we were able to provide papers for."[2] When news of a Jew being detained by Nazis reached Sanz Briz, he would call the *Gauleiter*. The detainee would then be escorted to the Spanish buildings and released to find sanctuary there.

Often Sanz Briz interceded to keep Jews from being sent on forced marches to the Austrian border. Sometimes he went to the line of march and secured the release of Jewish prisoners by insisting that they were Spaniards. All in all, Angel Sanz Briz is credited with saving more than 5,200 Jews from the Holocaust.

The Samurai Code

One of the foreign consuls most dedicated to thwarting the Holocaust was Chiune Sugihara, who represented the Japanese government in Kaunas, the temporary capital of Lithuania, from March 1939 through September 1, 1940. Born in 1900, Sugihara had been raised in the tradition of the samurai, a Japanese warrior class with a strict code of honor. He took to heart the old samurai saying that "even a hunter cannot kill a bird which flies to him for refuge."[3]

After joining the Japanese foreign ministry, Sugihara was sent to Manchuria to serve with the government installed by the Japanese after their successful invasion of that Chinese province. He negotiated the purchase of the Manchurian railroad system from the Russians who had built it, and was promoted to vice minister of the Foreign Affairs Department. He was in line to become minister of foreign affairs in Manchuria. However, before that could happen he resigned his post in protest against the inhumane treatment of Chinese civilians by the Japanese army. Indignation at his defiance may have been the reason why, five years later, he was assigned to run the relatively unimportant one-man consular office in Kaunas.

Chiune Sugihara

His arrival in Kaunas corresponded with the beginning of the arrival of Polish-Jewish refugees in that city. With the German invasion of September 1939, the trickle of refugees turned into a deluge. Eyewitness accounts of mass murders were heard everywhere. In addition to the refugees, a quarter of the 120,000 residents of Kaunas were Jewish Lithuanians.

The Defiant Humanist

The Russians, at that time still allied with the Germans, seized the city in June 1940. They announced that they would allow Polish Jews to leave Lithuania via Russia if they had authorized travel documents. Thousands of refugees descended on the Japanese consulate pleading for transit visas. However, in July the Russians ordered all foreign embassies to clear out of Kaunas. Refusing to go, Chiune Sugihara was one of the only two foreign consulate officials to remain. The other was Jan Zwartendijk, the acting consul of the Netherlands. Using information provided by Zwartendijk, Sugihara hatched a plan to rescue the Jews trapped in Kaunas.

Two Dutch Caribbean islands, Curaçao and Dutch Guiana, did not require formal entrance visas. In order to reach them from Lithuania via Russia, however, the refugees would have to travel east. To the west there were only Nazis and the initial slaughtering of the Jews. Going east meant they would have to cross the vastness of Russia and then pass through Japan. They would require transit visas from the Japanese consul.

Sugihara wired Tokyo for permission to grant the visas. Three times he was turned down. The last time the foreign ministry telegraphed him that "TRANSIT VISAS . . . ABSOLUTELY NOT TO BE ISSUED."[4]

Knowing that he was putting his diplomatic career at risk, Sugihara defied the foreign ministry. For four weeks in August 1940, he and his wife, Yukiko, wrote and signed visas, registering them carefully for the foreign office, which had ordered him not to issue them. They wrote more than three hundred visas every day. Then they handed them out to those who were standing in line day after day in front of the consulate.

On September 1, 1940, Sugihara was forced to leave Kaunas on a train bound for Berlin. From the window of the train he continued handing out transit visas to refugee Jews. As the train was pulling out of the station, he handed the consulate's visa stamp to a refugee with instructions to forge his signature when the stamp was used to create still more transit visas.

Sugihara was in disrepute with the Japanese foreign ministry, but the war was still on, Germany was an ally of Japan's, and experienced consular officers were in short supply. In 1945, after the Soviet Union declared war on Japan and just as hostilities in Europe were ending, he was arrested by the Russians as an enemy alien. Along with his wife and three children, Sugihara spent sixteen months in a Soviet prison.

When Sugihara and his family were released, he returned to Japan. He was greeted with a demand that he resign from the diplomatic service. The reason given was "the incident in Lithuania." Chiune Sugihara's career was shattered. That was the price this truly noble samurai paid for saving the lives of thousands of Polish and Lithuanian Jews.[5]

t the beginning of the Holocaust, the Jews could not believe that the Nazis were actually going to exterminate them. Yes, they were being persecuted, but they had been persecuted before in Germany, Poland, Hungary, Austria, France, Russia, and many other European countries. Their rights had been curtailed by law, they had been insulted, there had been pogroms, and they had been expelled from their homes. But to wipe out all the Jews in Europe? How could such a thing be done? It seemed impossible.

The Protection of Loved Ones

This disbelief worked against the Jews. It hindered any effort to organize to protect themselves. Also, the Jews existed as relatively small minorities in Nazi-controlled countries, and there was no establishment to coordinate action among such groups. There was no Jewish armed force at the start of the Holocaust. Mostly there were families with old people and children and hardworking parents with not enough money to bribe their way to freedom. They were slow to defend themselves, lest punishment fall on their loved ones.

In cities and towns Jews turned to their religious leaders to bring some sort of sense and order to their situation. To avoid chaos and confusion, these leaders drew up lists and worked out schedules for departures from Nazified areas.

The Nazis used the lists to round up Jews. They told the Jews many lies, including that they were being transported to Poland to settle in farming country, and that they would be given land. Instead, the trains took them to their death.

It was only with the realization of the true horror of their situation that Jews fought back. Some individuals reacted irrationally. One who did was an unstable seventeen-year-old youth named Herschel Grynszpan.

Expulsion and Assassination

Herschel Grynszpan was a student in Paris and the son of Polish Jews who had lived in Hanover, Germany, for twenty-seven years. His father, Zindel Grynszpan, ran a grocery store there. On October 27, 1938, at eight o'clock in the evening, Zindel Grynszpan and his family were taken from their home.

The Nazis had decided to expel Polish Jews. Along with six hundred others, the Grynszpans were loaded into trucks and then onto trains bound for the Polish border. The streets and then the railway platforms were lined with Germans shaking their fists at them and shouting "*Juden raus* [Jews out] to Palestine!"[1]

At the border, in accordance with German law, all of their possessions and money save for ten marks was taken from the Grynszpans and each of the other Jewish families. SS men drove them across the border with whips. "Blood was flowing on the road," recalled Zindel Grynszpan. Their treatment by the Poles was little better. There was no food, and they were housed in stables. Grynszpan then wrote a letter to his son Herschel. "Don't write any more letters to Germany," he concluded. "We are now in Zbaszyn."[2]

Herschel went to the German Embassy in Paris to plead for his parents. The youth had grown up in Germany, and it made no sense to him that his family should be treated in this way. He was repeatedly denied access to the ambassador. Finally, Herschel came back with a pistol, which he fired at Ernst vom Rath, a low-level employee of the embassy, killing him. The assassination set off nationwide riots against Jews in Germany. History remembers them as *Kristallnacht* (Night of the Broken Glass) because of the thousands of windows of Jewish shops that were shattered.

He Died Fighting

A very different sort of resistance was offered by a Jew known only by his last name: Slapoberskis. The incident took place on August 28, 1941, in Kedainiai, Lithuania. Nazi security police, aided by civilian Lithuanians, had rounded up more than two thousand Jewish men, women, and children, and housed them in a barn. They then dug a pit in the woods, marched the Jews there in groups of two hundred, made them take off their clothes, lined them up at the edge of the pit, and killed them with machine-gun, rifle, and pistol fire.

The massively built Slapoberskis was ordered by a Lithuanian named Czygas to undress. Slapoberskis refused, reminding Czygas that he was a human being like him. Czygas, pistol in hand, began pulling off Slapoberskis's clothes.

The burly Jew grabbed the Lithuanian by the neck and jumped into the ditch with him. With his other hand, Slapoberskis got the gun away from Czygas and fired it at the Nazi in charge of the slaughter. When a German jumped into the ditch to help Czygas, Slapoberskis dropped the Lithuanian and began throttling the German. A second Lithuanian, Jankunas, came to the aid of the German only to find himself being strangled. Finally, Jankunas managed to pull a knife from his belt and stabbed Slapoberskis, killing him. Slapoberskis, however, had mortally wounded Czygas, who also died.

Poet and Martyr

Slapoberskis's resistance was the reaction of a man with nothing left to lose. Other Jews preplanned their bravery, often in terms of what was best for their people. This was particularly true of a young poet named Hannah Szenes.

A Hungarian Jew who became involved in Zionism, the struggle to establish a Jewish nation, she emigrated to Palestine (now Israel) in 1939. She lived on a kibbutz and wrote a play about life there, as well as several poems. When she was twenty-two years old, Szenes enlisted in the British army in order to fight Nazism. She volunteered for the paratroopers and was trained for three months in Egypt. Subsequently, she was one of thirty-three volunteers who were dropped into Nazi-occupied territory. Her assignment was to make contact with underground groups and organize help for Jews who were at risk.

Szenes joined up with Marshal Tito's partisans in Yugoslavia in March 1944. She spent three months with them, participating in sabotage, raids, and other anti-Nazi activities. During this time she wrote the poem *Blessed Is the Match,* a classic of Holocaust literature, which has been set to music.

When word reached the partisans of the June 1944 mass roundups of Hungarian Jews, Szenes left them and crossed the border into Hungary. Either through a foul-up, or possibly because she was betrayed, Hannah was apprehended by the pro-Nazi Hungarian police. Their first objective with her was to obtain information about her underground contacts in Hungary and Yugoslavia.

She was interrogated and tortured over a period of several months. She refused to name names or divulge any other information. She was warned that harm would come to her mother and other members of her family if she did not give up her colleagues in the underground. Still, Hannah Szenes refused to speak.

Finally, weak from her ordeal, she was brought to trial as an enemy spy. There she publicly disavowed the Nazis and insisted that her anti-Nazi acts were justified. Given the opportunity to plead for her life, she refused. She was found guilty and sentenced to death. Declining the offer of a blindfold, Hannah Szenes was executed by a firing squad on November 7, 1944. She was just twenty-three years old.

Not "Sheep to the Slaughter"

There were many young Jews who proved themselves as courageous as Hannah Szenes. "In all the ghettoes . . . and the other occupied lands in Eastern Europe," wrote Holocaust scholar Lucy S. Dawidowicz, "in the wake of the great wave of killings or deportations, the youth of the Jewish political movements began to organize armed resistance to the Germans."[3] The first Jewish young people's resistance organization was set up in Vilna, Lithuania, in January 1942. Others followed throughout Eastern Europe.

When the Germans rounded up Jews for deportation, they used them for labor before putting them to death. They wanted the able-bodied who could handle strenuous work. But as the Jews became aware that deportation led inevitably to death, often the old volunteered to be transported in order to spare the young. This was a major reason that youths were frequently the last ones left in a ghetto, and a factor in their organizing to fight what was frequently a hopeless battle.

Their determination was voiced by Abba Kovner, a Vilna resistance leader and poet. "We will not be led like sheep to the slaughter," he thundered.[4] The sentiment was repeated from ghetto to ghetto as young Jewish men and women took up arms against German tanks, cannons, and machine guns.

Mordecai Tennenbaum-Tamarof went from Vilna to Bialystok, Poland, to organize the resistance there. In a letter to his sister, he described the activities of his close companion, Tama Schneiderman, who gathered information and acted as a courier, slipping back and forth across Nazi lines to maintain contact among the Jewish resistance groups in various areas: "She was a living encyclopedia of the catastrophe and martyrdom of the Jews of Poland. . . . Whenever someone was caught in the camps—they had to be rescued! At the station, when a railway carriage is being suspiciously prepared, it was necessary to find out why, and where it was headed, and warn others to be careful. A fire in a village—money was needed there. Seek out partisans in the forest. Buy arms.

Everything."[5] On one such mission Tama Schneiderman vanished and was never heard from again.

The Battle of Bialystok

Following Schneiderman's disappearance, Tennenbaum-Tamarof continued building the resistance movement in Bialystok. There were 35,000 Jews in that ghetto, 14,000 of them used as slave labor in Nazi-run factories. In early 1943, the Nazis began rounding up nonworking Jews—mainly old people and children—in the Bialystok ghetto. One of these tossed acid into the eyes of a Nazi. The blinded officer fired a shot and killed one of his own men. Following the incident, hundreds of Jews were shot on the spot. Between eight thousand and ten thousand of those who survived the initial assault were shipped to death camps.

In August military units of German Nazis with Ukrainian helpers descended on the city. All Jews were ordered to report to a collection point for transport. Families were torn apart as the able-bodied were separated from the ailing, parents from their children, and husbands from their wives. Thousands were herded into a stockade where they waited—sometimes for days—under a blazing sun for the trains to arrive that would take them to the death camps.

Mordecai Tennenbaum-Tamarof ordered his resistance fighters into action. Hopelessly outnumbered and short of ammunition, they battled the Nazis at every turn. A young Jewish woman named Mika Datner led two squads of mostly teenage women against the Nazis. They opened fire on those guarding the stockade. Their aim was to create a gap in the fence through which the detainees might escape. The Germans and Ukrainians retaliated with heavy fire, which decimated Datner's force. They also turned their guns on the Jews inside the stockade, killing many of them.

Nevertheless, the Jewish insurgents kept on battling for four days. In the end, though, they were wiped out. Among those who died was resistance leader Mordecai Tennenbaum-Tamarof.

German soldiers survey Jewish casualties after the suppression
of the Warsaw ghetto uprising.

The Warsaw Ghetto

The best-known Jewish uprising was in the Warsaw ghetto. In 1940 the Nazis herded 400,000 Jews into a walled-in area of Warsaw 2.5 miles (4 kilometers) long and a mile wide. For the next two years with heating fuel, food, and medicine scarce, disease reached epidemic proportions, killing many people. Others died from starvation and exposure.

In July and August 1942, some 300,000 Warsaw ghetto Jews were either murdered outright or shipped in overcrowded boxcars to death camps such as Treblinka, where they were the first to die in that camp's new gas chambers. Only 60,000 Jews were left in the Warsaw ghetto. By January 1943, they had learned of the death camps. They weren't really organized, but when the Nazis started rounding up ghetto factory workers on January 18, the Jews fought back.

The first action was planned by Mordechai Anilewicz of the Jewish Combat Organization. His people joined the lines of Jews being herded to transport points. They positioned themselves close to those guarding the line. When Anilewicz gave the signal, the resistance fighters pulled out weapons and attacked the Nazi guards. Soon reserve troops reinforced the guards, and most of Anilewicz's fighters were driven off or killed. By then, however, the hundreds of Jews who had been in the line had run away and found hiding places.

The Nazis were shaken. Rounding up sick, starved ghetto Jews was considered easy duty compared with going into battle. Now some of them had died doing it. It was as if they could sense the spirit of resistance spreading through the Warsaw ghetto. The initial battle was followed by others in which the Jewish Combat Organization fought openly to rescue those rounded up by the Nazis. Commemorating these actions, a ghetto poet wrote a poem that ended with these lines:

Like a bouquet of blood-flowers
The heart cries out from the gun-barrels
This is our spring—our counterattack.[6]

There were dozens of German casualties. In putting down the counterattack, the Nazis murdered a thousand Jews. For the time being, though, the mass expulsion to the death camps had been halted.

The "Murder Expedition"

The Warsaw ghetto was now a thorn in the Nazis' side. *Reichsführer* Heinrich Himmler ordered that the ghetto be cleaned out entirely. He assigned the task to General Jürgen Stroop. On April 19, 1943, Stroop launched a "Murder Expedition"—as German General Alfred Jodl described it—against the Warsaw ghetto.[7] Stroop estimated that the operation would take three days.

Zionists, Communists, Gypsies, and other groups that formed spontaneously as events unfolded joined with the Jewish Combat Organization to battle Stroop's heavily armed troops. The Jews had obtained dynamite from the Polish underground, and they had mined key positions leading in and out of the ghetto. Initially, the dynamite turned back Stroop's tanks and artillery vehicles. What followed is described by Tuvia Borzykowski, a survivor of the Warsaw ghetto: ". . . We did not wait for the enemy to be the first to start the slaughter, and from all our posts we showered a hail of bullets and hand-grenades and bombs. . . . they . . . did their work well, leaving many slain and wounded Germans on the streets."[8]

"Juden Haben Waffen!"

The Germans were unprepared for such resistance. The cry was sounded: *"Juden haben Waffen!"* (The Jews have arms!).[9] The Germans turned tail and withdrew. Over a house on Muranowska Street, the Jews raised a Zionist flag and a Polish flag.

General Stroop notified his superiors that his forces had come under attack. One of his tanks, struck by Molotov cocktails (bottles of gasoline with homemade fuses), had twice burst into flames. He reported twelve casualties. There may have been more that he didn't know about.

When he heard that the German soldiers had run away, *Reichsführer* Himmler was enraged. Under pressure, Stroop devised new tactics suitable for street fighting. Using a barricade of mattresses, the Germans attacked a house used as an observation post. When the house went up in flames, the Jews were forced to abandon it, but not before they set the Germans' mattresses on fire.

The Germans were stymied. No sooner would they capture or kill one band of resistance fighters than another would spring up to take its place. They were particularly bedeviled by the *Chaluzim,* Jewish women guerrilla fighters who were especially ferocious. They would attack, "firing pistols with both hands," and when captured they would pull the pins on hand grenades concealed in their underwear so that their captors might die with them.[10]

The Passover Seder

Stroop brought in flamethrowers and began burning down the buildings held by resistance fighters. The soldiers wielding the flamethrowers came under heavy sniper fire from the rooftops of nearby buildings. Nevertheless, many of the resistance fighters were burned alive. Others fought their way out and escaped to underground passageways and sewers.

The sewer fighters were particularly dangerous to the Nazis. There were manholes everywhere, and suddenly a head would pop up, there would be a burst of bullets, dead and wounded soldiers, and before the Germans knew what hit them, the guerrilla would close the manhole cover and vanish from sight. When the Germans tried to flood the sewers, the Jews attacked in force, seized control of the valves, and stopped the flooding. Nor were smoke bombs effective in stopping attacks from the sewers.

The battle in the streets, sewers, and rooftops continued through the start of the Jewish holiday of Passover. Surrounded by burning houses and the sounds of gunfire, Rabbi Meisel held a seder for some of the young ghetto fighters. They dined by sparse candlelight, and as they left to resume the fighting, the rabbi spoke to them from the shadows. "I am old," he said, "but you are youngsters; do not be afraid, fight and succeed. And may God go with you."[11]

"Blow It Up"

As casualties mounted, General Stroop brought in artillery to shell the area. "I decided to evacuate the whole sector by force, or to blow it up," he recorded later.[12] A total of 4,675 Polish slave laborers were escorted into the ghetto by armed guards and put to work clearing away the walls of buildings still left standing, as well as any piles of rubble that might be used as cover for sniper fire. As they worked, the battle went on around them.

Facing more and more German force, and with fewer places to hide, the resistance was now a doomed cause. Many fighters engaged in suicide missions, attacking Germans and killing one or two before succumbing to overwhelming numbers. Their heroism was to no avail in what had now become for Stroop's forces a mop-up operation.

By May 16, 1943, the battle of the Warsaw ghetto was over. Stroop had said it would take three days to clear the ghetto. It took a month. He recorded the "total number of Jews dealt with: 56,065, including both Jews caught and Jews whose extermination can be proved."[13] General Stroop received the Iron Cross First Class, Germany's highest medal, for carrying out the so-called Murder Expedition. The Jews who died fighting his forces in the last days of the Warsaw ghetto received no medals, but their heroism will not be forgotten.

THE
DEATH CAMP
REBELLIONS

Among the Jews rounded up and deported from the Warsaw ghetto following the uprising were 1,700 who were sent to the Bergen-Belsen concentration camp. They were told by the Nazis that they would be taken from there to Switzerland. Instead, they were transported to Auschwitz where, on October 23, 1943, they were herded to the gas chambers.

About two thirds of the prisoners had already undressed and entered the gas chambers when those still in the undressing room rebelled. What followed was described in March 1946 at the Nuremberg war crimes trial by the notorious commander of Auschwitz, Rudolf Hoess: "Three or four armed SS noncommissioned officers entered the room to speed up the undressing. The electric wires were cut, the SS men were attacked and deprived of their weapons, and one of them was stabbed to death. Since the room was now completely dark, there was a wild shootout between the guards at the entrance and the prisoners inside. When I arrived, I ordered the doors shut and the gassing process of the first two thirds stopped. Then the guards and I entered the room with handheld searchlights and we herded the inmates into a corner, from where they were led out individually and upon my orders shot with small-bore rifles in a room next to the crematorium."[1] Many of these individuals continued to resist right up to the moment of their death.

One of those killed by the doomed Jews was an SS officer named Schillinger whose cruelty as roll-call officer made him one of the most hated Germans in the camp. It was said that he had tried to rip off the bra of a woman in the undressing room. She wrestled his pistol from him and shot him.

The Depot Uprisings

The rebellion of the Warsaw ghetto prisoners at Auschwitz was not an isolated incident. There was resistance at all the death camps. It took many forms. Sometimes it started in the overcrowded boxcars before they even reached the camps. The deportees, jammed in to the point of suffocation, worked together to pull up the flooring so that some of them might escape by jumping to the tracks between the fast-moving wheels of the train. Sometimes they ripped out the barbed wire covering the air vents and pushed their children free. They yelled at them to run—run!—when the Nazi guards opened fire on them.

There were uprisings when the trains reached their destination. On April 30, 1943, arrivals at the Sobibor death camp attacked the Germans and Ukrainians guarding the railroad platform. Many of the guards were badly injured before the uprising was brought under control and the Jewish rebels were killed. Less than six months later another group of deportees from Minsk stormed out of the boxcars with sticks, stones, bottles, pots, and all sorts of homemade weapons to attack the Sobibor depot guards. They too went to their deaths fighting.

What may have been the first such incident occurred at the Treblinka camp in December 1942 when "a great riot began."[2] As two thousand Jews were being unloaded from the boxcars, a group of Jewish teenagers and young men already in the camp rushed the guards with knives and bare hands, shouting to the arrivals that the showers they were being taken to were really gas chambers where they would be killed. The newcomers joined the youths, and a pitched battle ensued. Weapons were seized from the guards, grenades were exploded, and the Ukrainians and Germans were overwhelmed. The Treblinka commander had to rush reinforcements to the depot to bring the riot under control. When that was done, all those involved were executed.

The Totenreserve

In all of the death camps there were prisoners who were kept alive in order to perform tasks necessary to the running of the institution. Sometimes these were people with special skills such as mechanics, electricians, nurses, or accountants. Sometimes they were those lucky enough to have been assigned as clerks or ward attendants or even gardeners, domestics, or nannies, in the service of a Nazi officer's family. Their positions sometimes allowed them to help other inmates.

Many risked their lives to do that. In Buchenwald, for instance, record keepers and hospital personnel started a *Totenreserve* (corpse bank). When a prisoner died or was killed, his or her name would be entered in the *Totenreserve*. When another prisoner would become scheduled for death, his name would be switched with that of the prisoner who was already dead. The living prisoner's name would appear on the list of prisoners already dead and would be crossed off the list of those slated for execution. In this way the living prisoner would escape his fate. According to later testimony, some 130 prisoners' lives were saved by the *Totenreserve*.

In Ravensbruck, inmate nurses saved the lives of some young people who had been crippled in experiments conducted by Nazi doctors. At great risk to themselves, they "were able to give a few of them the numbers of dead prisoners and place them on a transport leaving for a factory."[3] The nurses had also smuggled out information about these mutilating experiments to the Allies.

Helpers and Betrayers

On June 20, 1943, a letter to all concentration camp commandants stated that the increasing number of escapes made a very unfavorable impression on *Reichsführer* Heinrich Himmler. The letter went on to say that these escapes invariably took place with the help of other inmates. At Auschwitz this involved the establishment of hiding places for escapees within the camp until the guards had withdrawn from a specific area and they could make a break for it. If those involved in helping the escapees were caught, they were immediately hanged as an example to other inmates.

Escapes required money—or at least items of value, which could be used as barter. Such assets could be used to bribe guards and to obtain local currency, which could be used by escapees once they were outside the fences of the camps. Many such items were taken from the corpses of the victims of the gas ovens. It was the job of the prisoners assigned to the undressing rooms and the crematoriums to collect such items and sort them. These might range from cash sewed into clothing and hidden heirlooms to the gold fillings in the teeth of those slaughtered. It was relatively easy to siphon off items of value and use them for barter with the guards. According to Rudolf Hoess, at Auschwitz "the valuables of Jews caused the camp enormous and uncontrollable difficulties. . . . Money, watches, rings, etc., could be traded for anything with SS men and civilian workers."[4] They were also used to buy weapons and as bribes in arranging escapes.

Jews who escaped the death camps in Poland might then be faced with two possibilities. They might receive help and shelter from the local population and anti-German partisan groups. Or they might be hunted down and turned in by anti-Semitic Poles.

One group of Jews who had escaped from Sobibor encountered a Polish guerrilla band calling themselves the native army. They took the Jews' money and their only weapon and then chased them away. As the Jews fled, the Poles opened fire on them. Twelve of the fifteen Jews were killed.

On the other hand, members of a Polish family who hid an escapee were hanged for concealing him. Many Poles risked their lives to help Jews who had escaped concentration camps. Other Poles turned them in to the Nazi authorities.

"Sabotage Is Like Wine"

The Jews, Gypsies, and others in the death camps managed to stay aware of what was happening in the war. Parts were smuggled in, and radios were built

Roza Robota
(left) was the
leader of a
group of women
at the Birkenau
concentration
camp who suc-
ceeded in smug-
gling explosives
from an ammu-
nition factory
and blowing up
one of the
camp's gas
chambers.
Robota, along
with her three
conspirators,
was later caught
and hanged
publicly.

and hidden. New arrivals passed on information even as they were being marched to the gas chambers. The information was circulated throughout the camp.

One bit of information that went the rounds in 1942 was that Germany was running low on war supplies because of a labor shortage. It was learned that factories were being constructed next to the camps so that inmates could be used as slave labor. This actually meant an improvement in the inmates' condition, for if they were to work efficiently, they would have to be fed and cared for adequately. Also, they would be kept alive longer.

Nevertheless, these laborers were not eager to help the Nazi war effort. A phrase, Polish in origin, circulated among them: "Sabotage is like wine." And so they drank the wine of sabotage, mostly in moderation, but sometimes to excess.

As a rule, they merely slowed down or worked inefficiently. Sometimes they went further. In the Auschwitz motor pool, inmate mechanics regularly damaged the cars and trucks. At Sachsenhausen, instead of installing steel plates in the tanks they were assembling, the slave laborers mixed them in with the rubble that was being scrapped. Tools were misplaced, screws and washers were dropped into machines causing them to grind to a halt, deadlines were missed, airplane motors were disabled, and technicians deliberately built defects into aircraft engines.

Resistance groups organized sabotage tasks. It began with work assignments where those with special skills were deliberately given low-level jobs at which they wouldn't have to use their expertise. Others were deliberately positioned where their knowledge would help them commit sabotage. At Auschwitz, "work production declined by 50 percent within a few months after systematic sabotage had been organized."[5]

Undermining the Death Machine

Sometimes the sabotage had a more direct effect on the lives of the inmates. On May 9, 1942, at Dachau, an order was issued for inmates to build a large new crematorium with many ovens and a gas chamber. Inmate Karl Wagner, a German who was a mason by trade, was put in charge of those assigned to the project. "Comrades," he told them, "the gas chamber through which all of us may be intended to march must never be finished. . . . Sabotage wherever you can!"[6]

They did. Somehow the cement crumbled and refused to hold together. The foundation turned out not to be able to support the structure. The bricks were laid crookedly, and wall after wall had to be pulled down and put up again. It took so long to complete the crematorium that the building of the gas chamber was canceled.

There were similar acts at other camps. The crematoriums and the equipment for the gas chambers were often out of commission. Those who were apprehended for such acts might be tortured to name their accomplices. Always, in the end these brave people were killed.

Preparing for Rebellion

From the beginning there were those in the death camps who stood up and fought back. In Belzec, in June 1942, when Jews were assigned to dispose of the dead bodies of women and children, they revolted and killed half a dozen German guards before they were subdued. In September of that year, at Treblinka, a Jew named Meir Berliner, whose wife and daughter had just been killed in the gas chambers, jumped the Nazi officer in charge and killed him with a homemade knife. In August 1943, Treblinka inmates rose up against their guards with pitchforks, hoes, hammers, and sharpened screwdrivers, wrenching guns and grenades from them. They set fires and exploded the grenades at key positions, enabling some four hundred prisoners to break through the fence to freedom.

There are many such accounts. The best documented is a revolt led by a Russian Jew named Aleksander Pecherskii. A Red Army officer, he arrived at Sobibor on September 23, 1943. Shortly after his arrival, he was approached by a fellow inmate with an offer to help him escape. Pecherskii refused on the grounds that escapes by individuals would bring down reprisals on the prisoners remaining behind. However, he did believe that a mass escape would be justifiable.

Such an escape would be possible only during a rebellion by a large number of prisoners. Persuaded, the secret resistance group in the camp named Pecherskii its leader. Under his guidance they made plans for a major uprising.

Their first concern was obtaining weapons and warm clothing for those who would escape. A blacksmith prisoner surreptitiously made and distributed small, sharp axes, which could be hidden under clothing. Knives were smuggled out of the Germans' mess hall. Hand grenades and pistols were stolen by children who worked in the officers' quarters shining shoes and by women who scrubbed floors there. One sixteen year old who worked as a plumber concealed rifles in iron stovepipes, which he carried across the camp grounds for distribution to the rebels. Clothing was stolen by those who worked in the tailor shops. Many of those with jobs in camp workshops contributed to the preparation for the uprising.

Six Hundred Jews Attack

A schedule was worked out for October 14, the day of the uprising. The killing of Nazis would begin in the tailor and shoemaking shops. SS men had been told to come in at specific times for fittings or to pick up uniforms and boots. These pickups had been scheduled by the inmate workers in these shops at fifteen-minute intervals in midafternoon. The killings depended on German military punctuality.

The Germans were on time. Six top SS men, among them the deputy commandant of Sobibor, were killed in the fitting rooms. Four others were lured into a storeroom to try on the leather coat of a recent gassing victim and killed there. Another was slain in the garage. In all, eleven of the fourteen top camp officers were slain.

In late afternoon a German Jewish electrician named Schwarz disabled the camp electrical system and telephone lines. Things were going smoothly, but then an SS man discovered one of his dead comrades and opened fire on some inmates. Pecherskii immediately ordered that the signal be given for an attack on the camp arsenal.

A whistle was blown. Inmates rushed from all directions. In the vanguard, Pecherskii called out, "Comrades, forward!"[7] Initially, the guards were so stunned at the sight of six hundred Jews from Germany, Poland, France, Russia, the Netherlands, and Czechoslovakia storming the arsenal that they didn't react. But then they recovered, and the inmates were driven off by heavy machine-gun fire.

Machine guns were also being fired from the watchtowers now. Many of the inmates who rushed the fence were mowed down. Those who survived ripped at the barbed wire—no longer electrified—with their bare hands and created an escape hole. They fled across an open field. However, the field was mined. Those who went first were killed, but their bodies marked out a safe path for others to flee. One survivor wrote how he "was able to save my life by climbing to freedom over the dead bodies lying on the mines."[8]

Pecherskii led a group to the area of the officers' quarters. He believed they would not have laid mines just outside the fence there "because fragments might come in through the windows."[9] It was a good assumption. The prisoners were able to cut through the wire with shears. Many of them were killed by machine-gun fire while running through the open field beyond the fence, but some survived to reach the forest. Pecherskii was among them.

In all, some three hundred Jews escaped. About half of those who remained behind were shot immediately by the Germans. Most of the others died later in Sobibor.

They had fought the Nazis. Some had died fighting them. Some had given their lives so that others might survive. They had not gone passively to their deaths. On the contrary, they and many others in the death camps had answered the question that is so often asked about the Holocaust: Why didn't the Jews fight back?

The answer is that they did.

AFTERWORD

The Holocaust stands out in modern history as a record of inhumanity committed not in the heat of battle but in the calculated execution of helpless civilians. Old people were stripped naked and shot. Women were marched to the showers and killed in the gas chambers. Children went up in smoke in the crematorium ovens. Those responsible for these executions, and those who carried them out, are examples of the evil of which human beings are capable.

Their evil was horrible, but it is not unique. Even as it happened, it was not an evil peculiar only to the Germans, or even to the Nazis. There were people in almost every nation of Europe who collaborated in the Holocaust. There were people in every nation of the world who turned a deaf ear and a blind eye to it. There are people today who approve of it even as they attempt to claim that it never happened.

It happened. And the slaughter of the innocent did not end with the Holocaust. In the many years since World War II, helpless civilians—men, women, and children—have been massacred in Vietnam, Cambodia, Rwanda, Bosnia, Kosovo, Lebanon, Haiti, Afghanistan, Northern Ireland, Israel, Guatemala, Argentina, and many other countries. The potential for evil that the Holocaust demonstrates knows no national borders and no ethnic restrictions. It is universal.

The Heroes of My Lai

If the potential for evil is universal, however, then so is the potential for good. If there are people who take lives ruthlessly, there are also those who save lives and risk their own lives to do so. What was true during the Holocaust is true today. The evil is often transcended by the good, by the deeds of the brave and the unselfish who put humanity before self.

Hugh C. Thompson is such a person. More than twenty years after the Holocaust, he was flying a helicopter over the village of My Lai in South Vietnam when he and his two crew members spied U. S. soldiers gunning down unarmed civilians. Thompson landed his helicopter between a group of civilians—old people, children, and women—in a makeshift bunker and the GIs advancing on them. He confronted the soldiers and held them back with threats of a shootout. Thompson then called for another gunship to fly the GIs out of the area. Later, as Thompson's helicopter was flying off, crew member Glenn Andreotta detected movement in a ditch filled with bodies. They landed again and Andreotta retrieved a two-year-old child from the ditch. The child was still alive but covered with blood. Three weeks later Glenn Andreotta was killed in the line of duty in Vietnam.

A congressional committee investigating the My Lai incident found that American troops had "violated the law by slaughtering unarmed civilians by the hundreds."[1] Nevertheless, it wasn't until 1996, thirty years later, that Congress recognized Hugh Thompson's deed by awarding him the Soldier's Medal. The presentation of the medal was delayed for two years until March 1998. The reason was that Thompson would not agree to a private ceremony but insisted that the presentation take place at the Vietnam Veterans Memorial in Washington and that his two crew members—Glenn Andreotta and Larry Colburn—also be honored.

Why did Thompson intervene at My Lai? The answer he gave is not holier-than-thou or laced with sanctimonious language. His reason, he said, was simply that "what was going on wasn't right."[2]

The Truth Seeker

There is a reason that it took thirty years to honor Thompson and his crew. Doing so meant focusing attention on the massacre at My Lai and bringing shame on the United States and its fighting men. It is the same reason that the German nation for so many years tried to ignore the horrors of the Holocaust. The guilt and the shame felt in the aftermath of atrocities are not dealt with comfortably by nations and their people. Often those brave enough to confront their fellow citizens with the sins of the past may find themselves spat upon and their lives in danger.

This was the case of Anje Elizabeth Rosmus of Passau, Germany, a twenty-year-old student who in 1981 wrote a paper for an essay contest entitled "An Example of Resistance and Persecution—Passau, 1933–1939."[3] Her research hit a stumbling block when it came to the Jews of Passau. There were no records, no documents, no information available. Nobody wanted to talk about the Jews. The older people all insisted there was nothing to be said.

Rosmus placed an ad in a German-language Jewish newspaper in New York City. Soon the stories came pouring in. She checked them and cross-checked them. She went through the records gathered for the trials of Nazis following the war. She examined long-lost papers in national archives.

The facts she pieced together sickened her, but the horrors they revealed convinced her that they must be made public. She had learned that the mayor of Passau, who had always claimed to be a resistance fighter, was actually a Nazi party member. So, too, was the local priest. The citizens of Passau had taken over Jewish businesses and Jewish homes. They had rounded up the Jews and deported them. Horror stories abounded. Rosmus became convinced that those responsible should be punished. She exposed them all.

Her life was threatened. Her home was firebombed. The university she attended expelled her. Her young husband pleaded with her to stop, and when she wouldn't, he divorced her. She was a pariah in the town.

Eventually, Anje Elizabeth Rosmus prevailed. She received an official apology from the German government for having been thrown out of the university. A film was made about her struggle to make Passau face its role in the Holocaust. Today, the town invites a Jewish survivor to return each year as an honored guest. Most importantly, the case of Anje Elizabeth Rosmus received such wide attention internationally that the German government was forced to take steps to include Holocaust studies in German schools as part of the World War II curriculum.

Shielding the Enemy

Such Holocaust studies reveal the dangers of mob psychology. It is easier to kill helpless people when one is part of a group engaged in such activity. The individual conscience is drowned in the blood lust of the mob. To stand apart as an individual is difficult. To take action against a group bent on murder is the height of bravery.

Sometimes the source of such bravery is unexpected. Bella Freund was a forty-year-old woman with eight children when she heard shouts of "Terrorist!" and "Arab!" in a Jerusalem shopping center on a June day in 1991.[4] She was also an Orthodox Jew belonging to a strict sect called *haredim*. Wives of *haredim* are pledged to be submissive, to remain in the background, not to reveal emotion, or take action publicly.

An Arab had stabbed a Jewish boy, wounding him slightly. There were shots, and now the Arab was lying on the ground. A mob was assembling, bent on kicking and beating him to death. Somehow Freund pushed through the mob and flung her body over that of the Arab to shield him. Immediately the mob screamed names at her, calling her "Arab-lover," and showered blows on her.[5] The mother of the wounded Jewish boy cursed her. Later the mother said she was more furious at Freund than at the Arab.

Why did Freund do it? Why did she protect a would-be murderer against those bent on punishing him? Bella Freund was the child of Holocaust survivors. She could not understand the anger still directed against her long after the incident was over. "I protected someone because he was a human being," she explained.[6]

No other explanation is necessary. It is the most compelling lesson of the Holocaust. It is the duty of each and every one of us. Human life is sacred. It must be protected.

CHRONOLOGY

1918—November 11—World War I ends with the defeat of Germany.

1919—June 28—The Treaty of Versailles is signed.

1919—Adolf Hitler joins the Nazi party.

1919–1923—Anti-Semitism is on the rise in Germany.

1923–1924—Hitler writes *Mein Kampf*.

1933—Hitler becomes chancellor of Germany; first concentration camps are built; first anti-Jewish laws are passed.

1934—May—The Confessing Church is founded in Germany to oppose Hitler.

1935—September 15—Anti-Semitic Nuremberg laws are passed.

1936—March 7—German army occupies the Rhineland.

1938—Herschel Grynszpan, a seventeen-year-old Jew outraged at his family's forced expulsion from Germany, kills a German embassy official in Paris.

1938—German army invades Austria.

1938—November 9–10—*Kristallnacht*: Jewish shops are vandalized; synagogues are destroyed.

1938—Dominican Republic offers sanctuary to Germany's oppressed Jews.

1939—September 1—Nazi troops invade Poland; World War II begins.

1939–1940—Japanese Consul Chiune Sugihara saves thousands of refugee Polish and Lithuanian Jews in Kaunas, Lithuania, by handing out travel visas in defiance of his government.

1940—June—Nazi troops occupy Denmark, Norway, the Netherlands, Belgium, and western Poland; France surrenders; Nazis control most of Europe.

1940–1945—Five thousand villagers of Le Chambon-sur-Lignon, France, defy the Nazis to hide Jewish refugees and help them escape.

1941—July—Göring orders the "final solution of the Jewish question."

1941–1942—July–March—One million Jews are murdered, mostly by firing squads made up of SS troops, German Order Police, and non-German "helpers."

1942–1945—Zegota (Council for Aid to Jews) operates underground in Poland.

1942—June—Jews assigned to dispose of dead bodies at Belzec death camp rebel and kill six guards.

1942—July—Finland's Commander in Chief Carl Gustaf von Mannerheim threatens war if Germany so much as touches any of Finland's Jews.

1942—December—Jewish teenagers and young men rebel at Treblinka death camp.

1943—Danes ferry their Jewish population to neutral Sweden to save them from Nazis.

1943—The fury of the Warsaw ghetto rebellion led by Jewish resistance fighters stuns the Germans and arouses the admiration of the world.

1943—April—Jewish arrivals at Sobibor death camp attack German and Ukrainian guards.

1943—August—Mordecai Tennenbaum-Tamarof leads Jewish resistance fighters against Nazis in Bialystok, Poland, rebellion.

1943—October—Prisoners rebel while undressing for gas chambers at Bergen-Belsen death camp.

1944–1945—June–April—Swedish Consul Raoul Wallenberg saves the lives of thousands of Hungarian Jews.

1944—Spanish Consul Angel Sanz Briz saves more than five thousand Hungarian Jews by claiming them as Spanish nationals.

1944—Father Brunacci of Assisi, Italy, is arrested and exiled for shielding Jews from Nazis.

1944—November 7—Zionist poet-playwright Hannah Szenes, age twenty-three, is executed by a Nazi firing squad for her underground activities.

1945—April 9—Anti-Nazi German Pastor Dietrich Bonhoeffer is executed.

1945—April—Germany is defeated; the war in Europe ends.

1968—March—Helicopter pilot Hugh C. Thompson and his crew rescue Vietnamese villagers from slaughter by American soldiers.

1991—June—Bella Freund, Orthodox Jewish mother of eight, throws her body over an Arab terrorist to keep an angry Jerusalem crowd from beating him to death.

1998—March—Hugh C. Thompson and his crew are awarded the Soldier's Medal for heroism at My Lai.

CHAPTER NOTES

Chapter One

1. Eva Fogelman, *Conscience & Courage: Rescuers of Jews During the Holocaust* (New York: Anchor Books/Doubleday, 1994), p. 161.
2. Daniel Jonah Goldhagen, *Hitler's Willing Executioners: Ordinary Germans and the Holocaust* (New York: Alfred A. Knopf, 1996), p. 85.
3. Ibid., p. 82.
4. *Encyclopaedia Britannica,* vol. 8 (Chicago: Encyclopaedia Britannica, Inc., 1984), p. 253.
5. William L. Shirer, *The Rise and Fall of the Third Reich: A History of Nazi Germany* (New York: Simon & Schuster, 1960), p. 964.
6. Goldhagen, p. 149.

Chapter Two

1. Eric Silver, *The Book of the Just* (New York: Grove Press, 1992), p. 158.
2. Eva Fogelman, *Conscience & Courage: Rescuers of Jews During the Holocaust* (New York: Anchor Books/Doubleday, 1994), p. xvi.
3. Louis L. Snyder, *Hitler's German Enemies* (New York: Hippocrene Books, 1990), p. 12.
4. Ibid.

5. Susan Pottinger, *Life Magazine Hall of Heroes*, and *United States Holocaust Memorial Museum*. Internet address: www.us-israel.org/jsource/biography/schindler.html

6. Richard Z. Chesnoff, "The Other Schindlers" in *U.S. News & World Report,* March 21, 1994, pp. 56–64.

7. Ibid.

8. Raul Hilberg, *Perpetrators, Victims, Bystanders* (New York: HarperCollins, 1992), p. 220.

Chapter Three

1. Hannah Arendt, *Eichmann in Jerusalem: A Report on the Banality of Evil* (New York: Penguin Books, 1994), p. 188.

2. Ibid.

3. Ibid., pp. 187–188.

4. Ibid., p. 187.

5. Ibid.

6. Lucy S. Dawidowicz, *The War Against the Jews: 1933–1945* (New York: Holt, Rinehart and Winston, 1975), p. 373.

Chapter Four

1. Eva Fogelman, *Conscience & Courage: Rescuers of Jews During the Holocaust* (New York: Anchor Books/Doubleday, 1994), p. 148.

2. Ibid., p.149.

3. Eric Silver, *The Book of the Just* (New York: Grove Press, 1992), p. 19.

4. Ibid.

5. Ibid., p. 20.

6. Ibid., p. 119.

7. Istvan Deak, "Holocaust Heroes" in the *New York Review of Books,* November 5, 1992, pp. 22–26.

8. Anna Kassof, *Varian Fry and the Emergency Rescue Committee: A Resource Guide for Teachers* (Washington, DC: United States Holocaust Memorial Museum). Internet address: www.almondseed.com.vfry

Chapter Five

1. Raul Hilberg, *Perpetrators, Victims, Bystanders* (New York: HarperCollins, 1992), p. 224.
2. Eric Silver, *The Book of the Just* (New York: Grove Press, 1992), p. 131.
3. Alan Riding, "Marek Halter's Search for the 'Righteous' of Nazi Europe" in the *International Herald Tribune*, January 4, 1995. Internet address: dept.english.upenn.edu/~afilreis/holocau...dler010595.html
4. Istvan Deak, "Holocaust Heroes" in the *New York Review of Books,* November 5, 1992, pp. 22–26.

Chapter Six

1. Author not credited, "Other 'Schindlers' Revealed" in *World Press Review*, November 1994, pp. 44–46.
2. Ibid.
3. AICE: The Jewish Student Online Research Center (Jsource). Internet address: www.us-israel.org^source/holocaust/sugihara.htpl Excerpted from *Visas for Life* by Ron Greene, 1997.
4. Ibid.
5. *Chiune & Yukiko Sugihara: A True Story.* Internet address: http://vc.apanet.org/~visas/sugihara2.html

Chapter Seven

1. Hannah Arendt, *Eichmann in Jerusalem: A Report on the Banality of Evil* (New York: Penguin Books, 1994), p. 228.

2. Ibid., p. 227.

3. Lucy S. Dawidowicz, *The War Against the Jews: 1933–1945* (New York: Holt, Rinehart and Winston, 1975), p. 311.

4. Israel Gutman, *Resistance: The Warsaw Ghetto Uprising* (Boston: Houghton Mifflin Company, 1994), p. 104.

5. Ibid., p. 127.

6. Ibid., p. 184.

7. Ibid., p. 203.

8. Ibid., p. 205.

9. Ibid., p. 207.

10. William L. Shirer, *The Rise and Fall of the Third Reich: A History of Nazi Germany* (New York: Simon & Schuster, 1960), p. 976.

11. Gutman, p. 211.

12. Ibid., p. 214.

13. Shirer, p. 978.

Chapter Eight

1. Hermann Langbein, *Against All Hope: Resistance in the Nazi Concentration Camps, 1938–1945* (New York: Paragon House, 1994), p. 280.

2. Yitzhak Arad, *Belzec, Sobibor, Treblinka: The Operation Reinhard Death Camps* (Bloomington: Indiana University Press, 1987), p. 255.

3. Langbein, p. 203.

4. Ibid., p. 221.

5. Ibid., p. 306.

6. Ibid., p. 304.

7. Ibid., p. 299.

8. Ibid., p. 300.

9. Ibid.

Afterword

1. Trent Angers, *Hugh Thompson Jr. of Broussard, La.* Internet address: http://www.acadianhouse.com/hughthompson/story.htm

2. Ibid.

3. Eva Fogelman, *Conscience & Courage: Rescuers of Jews During the Holocaust* (New York: Anchor Books/Doubleday, 1994), p. 317.

4. Ibid.

5. Ibid.

6. Ibid., p. 320.

GLOSSARY

anti-Semitism—irrational hatred and persecution of Jews

Aryans—supposed Indo-Iranian ancestors of Germans on whom Nazis based their master-race claims

concentration camp—place of confinement for Jews and anti-Nazis; workplace; slaughterhouse

Confessing Church—anti-Nazi Protestant denomination formed in Germany in 1934

Death Books—Nazi records of numbers of Jews killed each day in the camps

death camps—concentration camps equipped for mass killing

final solution—the Nazi plan to kill off the entire Jewish population of Europe

gas vans—trucks with sealed compartments used to murder victims by carbon monoxide fumes

genocide—the killing of a whole race, people, or nation

Gestapo—Nazi secret police active in rounding up Jews for the death camps

ghetto—originally, a sealed-off area where Jews were forced to live

guerrilla—volunteer member of a small group fighting the occupying Nazi army

Holocaust—systematic extermination of six million European Jews by the Nazis

Judenrein—free of Jews

Mein Kampf (My Struggle)—Hitler's blend of autobiography and anti-Semitic call to arms

National Socialist German Workers Party—the Nazis

Order Police—reserve police units who helped round up and kill Eastern European Jews

pogrom—organized massacre of Jews in czarist Russia

Protocols of the Learned Elders of Zion—document forged in 1897 by Russian secret police to foment pogroms against Jews

Righteous Persons—non-Jews honored by Yad Vashem for saving Jews from the Holocaust

Schutzmannschaft—volunteers in Nazi-occupied countries who helped the SS slaughter Jews

Schutzstaffel (SS)—Hitler's personal guard unit; expanded in the war to perform mass killings

slave laborers—Jewish, Polish, Czech, and other prisoners forced to work in German industry

Treaty of Versailles—harsh terms imposed on Germany following defeat in World War I

Untermenschen—groups the Nazis labeled as less than human

Yad Vashem—Jerusalem Holocaust Memorial Museum

yellow star—a badge Nazis forced Jews to wear for ready identification

Zegota—Polish Council for Aid to Jews; an underground anti-Nazi organization during the war

Zionist—one favoring the establishment of a Jewish nation

Zyklon-B—the crystals from which the gas was made for mass killings in the death camps

FOR MORE INFORMATION

Arad, Yitzhak. *Belzec, Sobibor, Treblinka: The Operation Reinhard Death Camps.* Bloomington: Indiana University Press, 1987.

Browning, Christopher R. *Ordinary Men: Reserve Police Battalion 101 and the Final Solution in Poland.* New York: HarperCollins, 1992.

Fogelman, Eva. *Conscience & Courage: Rescuers of Jews During the Holocaust.* New York: Anchor Books/Doubleday, 1994.

Frank, Anne. *Anne Frank: The Diary of a Young Girl.* New York: Pocket Books, 1953.

Gilbert, Martin. *The Boys: Triumph Over Adversity.* London: Weidenfeld & Nicolson, 1996.

Gutman, Israel. *Resistance: The Warsaw Ghetto Uprising.* Boston: Houghton Mifflin Company, 1994.

Heyes, Eileen. *Children of the Swastika: The Hitler Youth.* Brookfield, CT: Millbrook Press, 1993.

Keneally, Thomas. *Schindler's List.* New York: Simon & Schuster, 1982.

Langbein, Hermann. *Against All Hope: Resistance in the Nazi Concentration Camps, 1938–1945.* New York: Paragon House, 1994.

Opdyke, Irene Gut, and Jennifer Armstrong. *In My Hands: Memories of a Holocaust Rescuer.* New York: Random House, 1998.

Rosenberg, Maxine B. *Hiding to Survive: Stories of Jewish Children Rescued from the Holocaust.* New York: Clarion Books, 1994.

Shirer, William L. *The Rise and Fall of the Third Reich: A History of Nazi Germany.* New York: Simon & Schuster, 1960.

Silver, Eric. *The Book of the Just.* New York: Grove Press, 1992.

Snyder, Louis L. *Hitler's German Enemies.* New York: Hippocrene Books, 1990.

Spiegelman, Art. *Maus: A Survivor's Tale: My Father Bleeds History.* New York, Pantheon Books, 1986.

Spiegelman, Art. *Maus II: A Survivor's Tale: And Here My Troubles Begin.* New York, Pantheon Books, 1991.

Yoran, Shalom. *The Defiant: A True Story.* New York: St. Martin's Press, 1996.

Internet Sites

The United States Holocaust Memorial Museum
   www.ushmm.org

The Holocaust: An Historical Summary
   www.ushmm.org/education/history.html

Holocaust Resources on the World Wide Web
   www.fred.net/nhhs/html/hololink.htm

The Jewish Student Online Research Center (JSOURCE)
   www.us-israel.org/jsource/

Remembering the Holocaust
   yarra.vicnet.net.au/~aragorn/holocaus.htm

The Forgotten Hero of My Lai: The Hugh Thompson Story by Trent Angers
   www.acadianhouse.com/hughthompson/story.htm

Steven Spielberg Jewish Film Archive
   www.sites.huji.ac.il/jfa/jfavid.htm

About the film *Schindler's List*
   www.ravecentral.com/schindlerslist.html

Chiune and Yukiko Sugihara: A True Story
   www.vconline.org/visas/sugihara.html

INDEX